JUNGLE

Black-and-
white colobus
Colobus guereza

Kapok pod
and seeds
Ceiba pentandra

Abarema idic

Blue–and–
yellow macaw
Ara ararauna

Rainforest house
(South America)

White–lipped
tree frog
Litoria infrafronata

DK EYEWITNESS BOOKS

JUNGLE

Written by
THERESA GREENAWAY

Photographed by
GEOFF DANN

*Clerodendrum
splendens*

Climbing fern
Leptochilus decurrens

Medicinal
Heckel
chewstick
Garcinia kola

Medicinal
calabar beans
*Physostigma
venenosum*

Stone axe
(Guyana)

Dorling Kindersley

Spear (Guyana)

Pacu
Colossom.

DK

Dorling Kindersley

LONDON, NEW YORK, AUCKLAND, DELHI, JOHANNESBURG, MUNICH,
PARIS and SYDNEY

For a full catalog, visit

DK www.dk.com

Cassava
squeezer
(Guyana)

Project editor Miranda Smith
Art editors Andrew Nash & Sharon Spencer
Managing editor Simon Adams
Managing art editor Julia Harris
Production Catherine Semark
Picture research Kathy Lockley
Researcher Céline Carez

This Eyewitness ® Book has been conceived by
Dorling Kindersley Limited and Editions Gallimard

Published in the United States by
Dorling Kindersley Publishing, Inc.
95 Madison Avenue
New York, NY 10016
2 4 6 8 10 9 7 5 3 1

Dorling Kindersley books are available at special discounts for bulk purchases for sales
promotions or premiums. Special editions, including personalized covers, excerpts of
existing guides, and corporate imprints can be created in large quantities for specific needs.
For more information, contact Special Markets Dept., Dorling Kindersley Publishing, Inc.,
95 Madison Ave., New York, NY 10016; Fax: (800) 600-9098

Library of Congress Cataloging-in-Publication Data
Greenaway, Theresa
Jungle / written by Theresa Greenaway; photographed by Geoff Dann.
p. cm. — (Eyewitness Books)
Includes index.
1. Rain forests—Juvenile literature. 2. Rain forest ecology—Juvenile literature.
[1. Rain forests. 2. Rain forest ecology. 3. Ecology.] I. Title.
QH86.G73 2000 574.5'2642—dc20   94-7948
ISBN 0-7894-5897-7 (pb)
ISBN 0-7894-5896-9 (hc)

Color reproduction by Colourscan, Singapore
Printed in China by Toppan Printing Co. (Shenzhen) Ltd.

Serpent carved
paddle (Papua
New Guinea)

Passionflower
Passiflora sp.

Contents

Red–kneed tarantula
Brachypelma smithi

What is a rain forest?

TROPICAL RAIN FORESTS are perhaps the least understood and most valuable of the world's ecosystems. They are structurally complex, ages old, and have a climate that allows year-round growth. They contain a larger diversity of plants and animals than anywhere else on Earth – for example, there are 20–100 different kinds of trees in one acre of rain forest alone. These jungles have three layers – an evergreen canopy in the middle, a layer of smaller plants on the forest floor, and towering above the canopy, scattered taller trees known as emergents. The speed at which the vegetation grows and fills any gap or forest clearing impresses modern visitors as much as it did the early explorers. Rain forests all around the world are amazingly uniform in many respects. Similar niches on different continents have been filled by species that look alike but are unrelated.

COLOR IN THE CANOPY
Splashes of color in the canopy may indicate that a tree has burst into flower. It is just as likely that a flush of red, orange, pink, or white new leaves has unfurled.

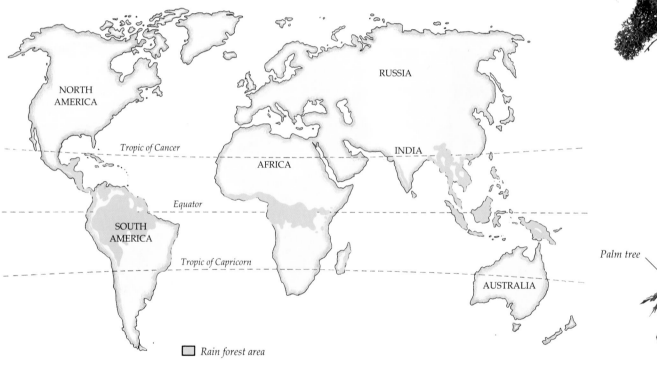

NORTH AMERICA

RUSSIA

Tropic of Cancer

AFRICA

INDIA

Equator

SOUTH AMERICA

Tropic of Capricorn

AUSTRALIA

Palm tree

☐ *Rain forest area*

Undergrowth

WARM AND VERY WET
Tropical rain forests are found in permanently wet, warm areas near the equator. There are at least 60 in (1,500 mm) of rain a year, with little or no dry season. The rain falls almost every day, in torrential downpours of huge raindrops. The average temperature is around 77°F (25°C), and there is little seasonal variation.

THE FOREST FLOOR
Swamp forest soils are regularly enriched by silt-laden floodwaters. Away from flooded areas, much of the lowland forest has surprisingly poor, infertile soils called oxisols. Nutrients are locked up in living plants and animals until released by organisms such as termites and fungi.

Tall emergent tree

Canopy

Liana

Young sapling

Green-winged
macaw

At the top

Black-and
white-colobus

Queen Alexandra's
birdwing

Forest canopy

Cuvier's toucan

White–lipped
tree frog

Forest floor

Red–kneed
tarantula

RAIN FOREST IN THREE STORIES
This model shows many of the features shared by all
lowland tropical rain forests. The trees have straight trunks,
with no branches for much of their height, and are supported by
buttress roots. Lianas, or climbing plants, twine up the trees, or begin life
lodged in the canopy and send roots down to the earth below. At ground
level, a luxuriant growth of plants springs up wherever the light reaches.

Tropical forests

THERE ARE SEVERAL different types of tropical forest. Lowland rain forest covers the greatest area and is found in the warm, wet lowland where there is little or no dry season. Tropical mountainsides are thickly forested. At altitudes over 3,000 feet (900 m), lowland rain forest changes to montane or high-altitude forest, which is divided i lower montane, upper montane, and cloud forest. Cloud forest begir at heights above 10,500 feet (3,200 m). At this altitude the stunted, gnarled trees are shrouded in mist and covered with mosses and liverworts. Sometimes the division between rain forest types is clear, but often two rain forest types merge so there is no clear boundary. Seasonal or monsoon forest – not technically rain forest – also has heavy rainfall, but there is a dry season of three months or longer, during which the trees shed their leaves. Lianas and epiphytes cannot survive these dry conditions.

MONTANE FOREST
In Malaysia, lowland rain forest gives way to lower montane forest at altitudes of about 3,000 ft (900 m). The climate is cooler but still moist. There is dense tree cover, but the height of the canopy gets lower and lower. The trees have smaller leaves, and tree ferns are abundant, as are magnolias, rhododendrons, myrtles, and laurels.

CLOUD F(
At higher altitudes, a permanent heav envelops the forest. The climate of forests, such as this reserve in Ecua cool and very damp. Moisture in the condenses on the surface of the leav constantly drips from them. Mosse liverworts cover everything with a s blanket. Because of the lower tempera the leaf litter decomposes very slov thick layer builds up on the gr eventually turning int(

Height at which montane forest replaces lowland forest is variable

Montane

Lowland

Mangrove

RAIN FOREST LEVELS
Lowland rain forest can extend down to the coast. Wherever conditions allow (p. 9), mangrove forest grows along the coast and in river estuaries. With every 330 ft (100 m) increase in altitude, there is a drop in temperature of about 1.1°F (0.6°C).

LOWLAND RAIN FOREST
The structure of th lowland rain fores Peru is clearly visi from the Rio de L(Amigos. In the foreground, youn climbers, ferns, an saplings flourish in the higher light levels beside the r A cycad, a remnar a truly ancient gro of plants, also grov in this clearing. Ta palms make up a l proportion of the canopy. The umbr shaped crowns of huge emergent tre tower above the ca

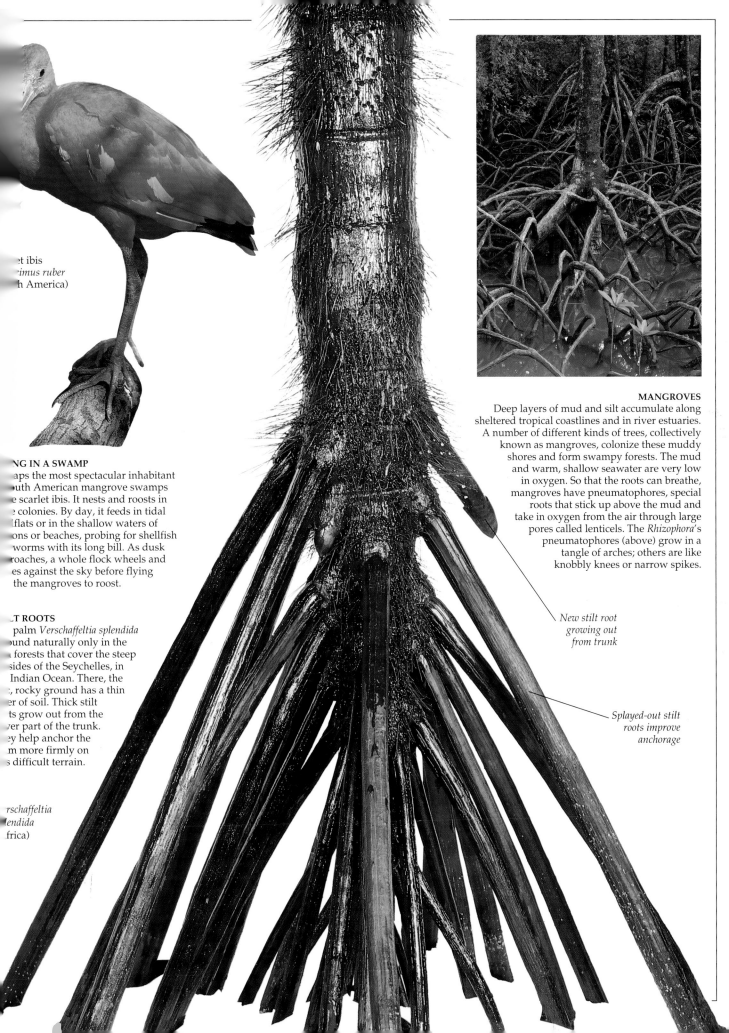

…et ibis
…imus ruber
…h America)

…NG IN A SWAMP
…aps the most spectacular inhabitant
…uth American mangrove swamps
…e scarlet ibis. It nests and roosts in
…e colonies. By day, it feeds in tidal
…flats or in the shallow waters of
…ons or beaches, probing for shellfish
…worms with its long bill. As dusk
…roaches, a whole flock wheels and
…es against the sky before flying
…the mangroves to roost.

…T ROOTS
…palm Verschaffeltia splendida
…ound naturally only in the
…forests that cover the steep
…sides of the Seychelles, in
…Indian Ocean. There, the
…rocky ground has a thin
…er of soil. Thick stilt
…s grow out from the
…er part of the trunk.
…y help anchor the
…m more firmly on
…difficult terrain.

…rschaffeltia
…endida
…frica)

MANGROVES

Deep layers of mud and silt accumulate along
sheltered tropical coastlines and in river estuaries.
A number of different kinds of trees, collectively
known as mangroves, colonize these muddy
shores and form swampy forests. The mud
and warm, shallow seawater are very low
in oxygen. So that the roots can breathe,
mangroves have pneumatophores, special
roots that stick up above the mud and
take in oxygen from the air through large
pores called lenticels. The *Rhizophora*'s
pneumatophores (above) grow in a
tangle of arches; others are like
knobbly knees or narrow spikes.

*New stilt root
growing out
from trunk*

*Splayed-out stilt
roots improve
anchorage*

At the top

TALL EMERGENT TREES tower above the rest of the jungle canopy, a few reaching heights of 200-230 ft (60-70 m). These scattered trees have straight trunks, often buttressed at the base, and a cauliflower-shaped crown. It is hotter and drier at the top of the canopy, and the temperature and humidity vary greatly. The trees are also much more windblown, and the fruit or seeds of some species are dispersed by the moving air. Many emergent trees are leafless for short periods of time, but seldom shed alltheir leaves at once. The epiphytes that live on the boughs of these trees include drought-resistant species of bromeliads, lichens, and cacti.

MONKEY BUSINESS
The striking black-and-white colobus monkey lives at the top of the jungle, feeding on leaves.

Sun conure
Aratinga solstitialis
(South America)

FLYING FORAGER
Conures live in noisy flocks high up in the treetops. They fly restlessly from tree to tree, feeding on flower buds, fruits, seeds, and insects.

PENANG FO
Tualang trees (*Koompassia exc*
often reach 230 ft (70 m) – t
285 ft (87 m) tualang holds the re
for the tallest broad-leaved rain fo
tree. Malaysians believe that sp
live in these t

Leaves have a waxy surface

GREEN SHADES
The tall canopy tree *Carapa guianensis* belongs to the mahogany family and is found predominantly in swampy or seasonally flooded parts of the forest. Mature trees may produce 300 or more large corky fruits that split into four segments, each containing two or three large seeds— most of which are eaten by animals.

Carapa guianensis
(Central and South America)

-EYED

rpy, one of the world's
eagles, leaves its
a tall emergent tree to
with speed and agility
h the canopy. With its
legs and immense
(its feet are the size of
's hands), it snatches
r monkeys or sloths,
hing them free from a
grasped branch. Harpy
use the same nest site
year. They build a bulky
sticks lined with leaves
r in the boughs of an
ent kapok tree, 165 ft
or so above the ground.

Harpy eagle
Harpia harpyja
(Central and South America)

Rhipsalis baccifera
(South America)

*Small
white fruit*

CACTUS AT THE TOP
Its fleshy, leafless stems
mean that this epiphytic
cactus can survive the long,
hot dry spells between
downpours. The small white
fruits have a sticky pulp that
helps them adhere to the bark.

ping leaf

Abarema idiopoda
(Central America)

Bi-pinnate leaf

LEAF DIVISION
Rain forest trees have
large leaves. These leaves
are either simple, with a
smooth outline and a
waxy surface, or
compound, when the leaf is divided into separate leaflets.
Abarema is bi-pinnate – its leaves are twice divided and have
small leaflets. *Carapa and Abarema* are leafless for brief
periods, when there is a dry spell, or the tree is flowering.

Forest canopy

IN THE CANOPY of a rainforest, 80-150 ft (25-45 m) above the ground, it is always green and leafy. The crown of each tree is taller than it is broad, making a sun-speckled layer 20-23 ft (6-7 m) thick. This leafy roof shields the ground and absorbs most of the sunlight. It also lessens the impact of heavy rainfall and high winds. The teeming life of a jungle canopy is only glimpsed from below. Some creatures are so adapted to their treetop existence that they seldom, if ever, descend to the forest floor. It is difficult even to match up fallen fruits or flowers with the surrounding tree trunks. Many species were totally unknown – or their numbers grossly underestimated – before walkways strung up in the canopy allowed biologists to find out what life was really like in the treetops.

LIFE IN THE CANOPY
This male tawny rajah (*Charaxes bernardus*) is one of many kinds of butterfly that may spend their entire life cycle up in the forest canopy.

SAFE ASLEEP?
Canopy-dwelling creat[ures] such as this silky or pyg[my] anteater (*Cyclopes didact[ylus]*) need to cling tightly to branches. Sharp claws a[nd] long prehensile (graspi[ng]) tail are adaptations share[d by] unrelated canopy anim[als].

REACHING THE HEIGHTS
Lianas are plants that need a lot of light and must compete with tall rain forest trees. By using these trees for support, the lianas do not invest energy and materials in a thick trunk of their own. Instead, their slender climbing stems reach the canopy, and the light, very quickly. Up among the branches, they loop through the treetops, growing leaves, flowers, and fruit.

Liana
Clerodendrum splendens
(Africa)

White-lipped tree frog
Litoria infrafrenata
(Australasia)

STICKY-TOED TREE TRAVELER
To avoid the hottest part of the day, thin-skinned tree frogs hide in damp leafy crevices among canopy epiphytes. The smaller tree frogs may spend their entire lives in the canopy, even breeding in the reservoirs of water trapped by bromeliad leaves. Others, such as this white-lipped tree frog, laboriously make their way down to forest pools to mate and spawn. Long legs and sticky toe pads enable them to climb with complete ease.

Cecropia glaziovii
(Central and South
America)

CANOPY FOLIAGE
The large leaves of lowland rain forest trees are
simple in shape, or are divided into leaflets like
this *Cecropia*. The canopy remains leafy all year,
but within it, some trees shed their foliage for
short intervals – sometimes as
little as a few days. Leaf-fall
usually coincides with the
driest time of the year,
but it is not always
synchronized,
even in trees of
the same
species.

*Leaf divided
into leaflets*

DRIP-TIPS
This typical rain forest leaf has
a shiny, waxy surface, and it
is drawn out into a narrow
point, or drip-tip. Both these
features are designed to
encourage rainwater to run
off quickly. This prevents
the growth of tiny algae
and liverworts.

*us religiosa
outheast Asia)*

FLEETING BEAUTY
Completely invisible from the ground,
epiphyte-laden boughs are like treetop
gardens. Of all the different plants
perched on these branches,
orchids are among the most
fascinating. The perfect
white orchids (right)
last just one day.

One-day orchid
Sobralia sp.
(Central America)

INSECT LIFE
Only some canopy insects have been
classified and named, like this click
beetle (*Chalculepidium* sp.). Even
then, little is known about them.

The forest floor

THE AIR NEAR the shady forest floor is still, hot, and humid. Only about two percent of the light reaching the canopy penetrates the thick blanket of foliage. This dim light inhibits the growth of tree seedlings and other light-demanding plants. In the deepest jungle, the ground is a maze of roots littered with fallen leaves, twigs, and branches. When a tree crashes down, the scene is very different – the extra light allows an upsurge of saplings, herbaceous plants, and lianas. Rates of growth are impressive; giant bamboo grows 9 in (23 cm) a day.

FOREST FUNGI
Bacteria, molds, and fsuch as this *Marasmius* quickly in the humconditions of the forest. A mass of fungal thr called a mycelium ta nutrients from the li of dead leaves, and brightly colored toads produce spores.

SHADE LOVER
Each long-stalked leaf of *Alocasia thibautiana* has silvery veins on top and is purple underneath. Clumps of these shade-loving aroids can grow in the gloomiest parts of Southeast Asian jungles – on the forest floor, beside streams, and even in the entrances of limestone caves.

A SPLASH OF COLOR
A luxuriant growth springs up wherever there is enough light. Heliconias, with their bright red flowerheads, are widespread in Central American jungles.

TRAPPING LIGHT
The leaves of *Fittonia* contain red pigments that trap the dim light that reaches the forest floor. Amerindian tribes use the plant to treat a variety of ailments.

Diplazium proliferum
(Southeast Asia)

Fittonia albivenis
(South America)

FLOURISHING
Ferns thrive best where it is warm and damp. Many tolerate low light levels, so they are abundant on the jungle floor. This fern produces bulbils on its fronds that will sprout and take root, either when they are knocked off or when the frond dies.

OWING WORM
ack-and-white amphisbaenid
isbaena fuliginosa) is neither a
nor a snake. It is a wormlike
sometimes called a worm lizard,
ves in burrows in the damp soil
af litter of the forest floor. It feeds
on worms and ants.

Banded pitta
Pitta guajana
(South America)

BROWSING BIRD
ng its good eyesight and
e of smell, the pitta forages
snails, ants, and other
nsects in the leaf litter.

TRESS ROOTS
e enormous roots are
acteristic of lowland
cal rain forest, where
s thin or subject to
ling. The curving
es rise from lateral
s. Buttress roots
spread up the
k to 30 ft
), forming
orting
s of
icularly
l wood.

In the water

THE RAIN FOREST is awash with water. It drips from the leaves, collects in puddles, runs down mountainsides, and eventually drains into huge, meandering rivers. The Amazon is the largest river of all – together with its tributaries, which number 1,000 or more, it holds two-thirds of the world's fresh water. This vast water system supports an incredible diversity of life. It contains around 5,000 species of freshwater fish, and there may be another 2,000 that have yet to be discovered. Where rain forest rivers flood, they spread nutrient-rich silts over the surrounding land, creating swamp forests. When they join the sea, more silt is deposited in estuaries and deltas, contributing towards mangrove swamps.

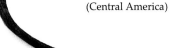

WELL CAMOUFLAGED
Lurking immobile in shallow water, the craggy carapace of the matamata (*Chelus fimbriatus*) looks like a rock. This Amazonian turtle has nostrils at the tip of its long, uptilted snout which is used like a snorkel as it lies in wait for prey.

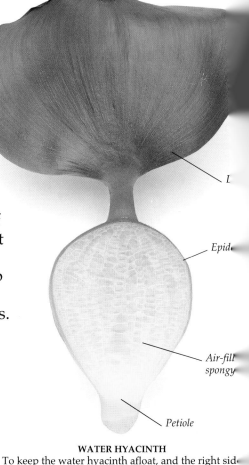

L

Epid.

Air-fill.
spongy

Petiole

WATER HYACINTH
To keep the water hyacinth afloat, and the right side up, the petiole (base) of each leaf stalk is swollen into an air-filled float. Cutting this in half reveals that each float is made up of a mass of air-filled spongy tissue. The leaf and stem are encased in a smooth, tough skin, called the epidermis.

RUNNING ON WATER
The Jesus Christ lizard, or basilisk, runs using its tail to balance itself. It has scales and a flap of skin on its hind toes to increase surface area, so it can run on *water* to chase prey or escape danger.

Long tail used as extra leg on land

Large back feet stop lizard sinking on water

Jesus Christ lizard
Basiliscus basiliscus
(Central America)

Pacu
Colossoma oculus
(South America)

FRUIT-EATING FISH
The varzea and the igapo are two areas of swamp forest flooded every year by the Amazon. Fruits falling from palms and other trees attract fish such as the pacu.

Water hyacinth
Eichhornia crassipes

DANGER IN THE WATER
Armed with fearsome rows of sharp, triangular teeth, the predatory piranha is dangerous only in the dry season, when water levels are low and the fish gather in schools of 20 or more. By feeding collectively, the fish are able to tackle large animals, although their usual prey is other fish, mollusks, fruits, or seeds.

Piranha
Serrasalmus niger
(South America)

FLOATING PLANT
The water hyacinth (above) floats with its feathery roots dangling down into the water. The plants grow very quickly, forming large rafts on the surfaces of lakes and slow streams. Smaller clumps are dispersed by the wind, blown along like small, unsinkable sailboats.

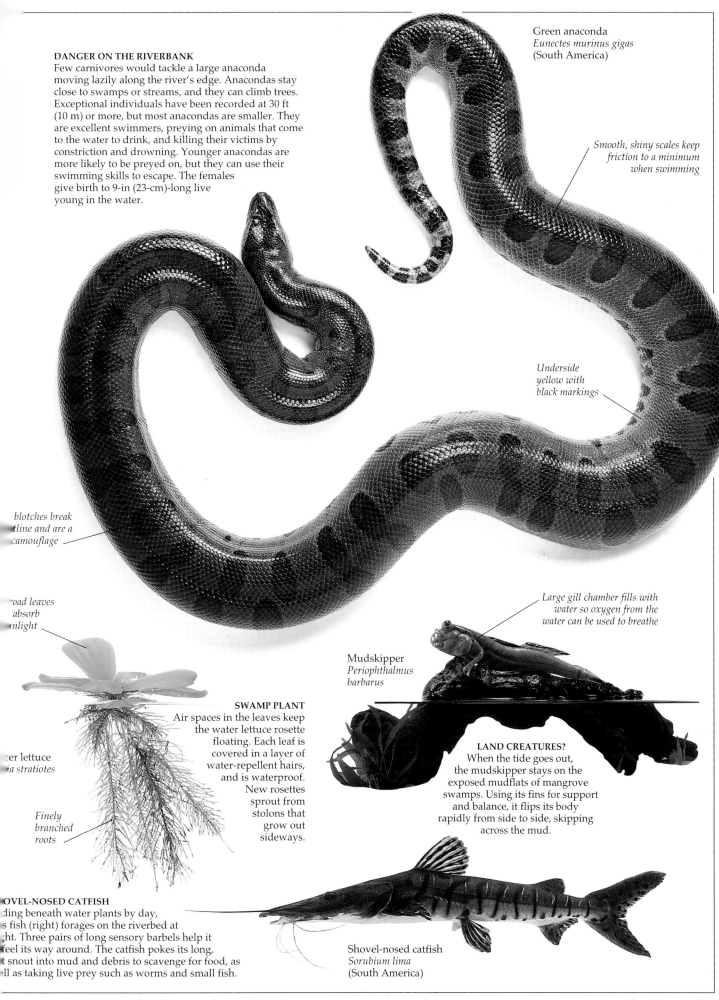

Green anaconda
Eunectes murinus gigas
(South America)

DANGER ON THE RIVERBANK
Few carnivores would tackle a large anaconda moving lazily along the river's edge. Anacondas stay close to swamps or streams, and they can climb trees. Exceptional individuals have been recorded at 30 ft (10 m) or more, but most anacondas are smaller. They are excellent swimmers, preying on animals that come to the water to drink, and killing their victims by constriction and drowning. Younger anacondas are more likely to be preyed on, but they can use their swimming skills to escape. The females give birth to 9-in (23-cm)-long live young in the water.

Smooth, shiny scales keep friction to a minimum when swimming

Underside yellow with black markings

blotches break [ou]tline and are a [good] camouflage

[Br]oad leaves [to] absorb [su]nlight

*[Wate]r lettuce
[Pisti]a stratiotes*

SWAMP PLANT
Air spaces in the leaves keep the water lettuce rosette floating. Each leaf is covered in a layer of water-repellent hairs, and is waterproof. New rosettes sprout from stolons that grow out sideways.

Finely branched roots

Large gill chamber fills with water so oxygen from the water can be used to breathe

Mudskipper
Periophthalmus barbarus

LAND CREATURES?
When the tide goes out, the mudskipper stays on the exposed mudflats of mangrove swamps. Using its fins for support and balance, it flips its body rapidly from side to side, skipping across the mud.

[SH]OVEL-NOSED CATFISH
[Hi]ding beneath water plants by day, [thi]s fish (right) forages on the riverbed at [nig]ht. Three pairs of long sensory barbels help it [f]eel its way around. The catfish pokes its long, [fla]t snout into mud and debris to scavenge for food, as [we]ll as taking live prey such as worms and small fish.

Shovel-nosed catfish
Sorubium lima
(South America)

Epiphytes

Up in the rain forest treetops, a special group of plants clothe the branches so thickly that the bark is hidden. These are called epiphytes—plants that live on other plants. They anchor themselves to the stems, trunks, branches, or even leaves of other plants. They do not take either water or food from their hosts. Instead, they use them as a means of reaching the light. After heavy rain, the combined weight of epiphytes and the water they have trapped can be enough to bring down whole branches. In the wettest forests, up to 25 percent of flowering plants and ferns are epiphytes, and there are many more kinds of mosses, liverworts, and lichens. The highest number of epiphytic species are found in Central and South American forests.

PLATYCERIUM
The bracket fronds of this large epiphytic fern loosely clasp the tree trunk, so that a litter of plant debris collects behind it. This compost is moistened by rainwater trickling down the trunk, and a rich humus develops into which the fern grows roots. Hanging clear of the trunk are the fertile, spore-bearing fronds.

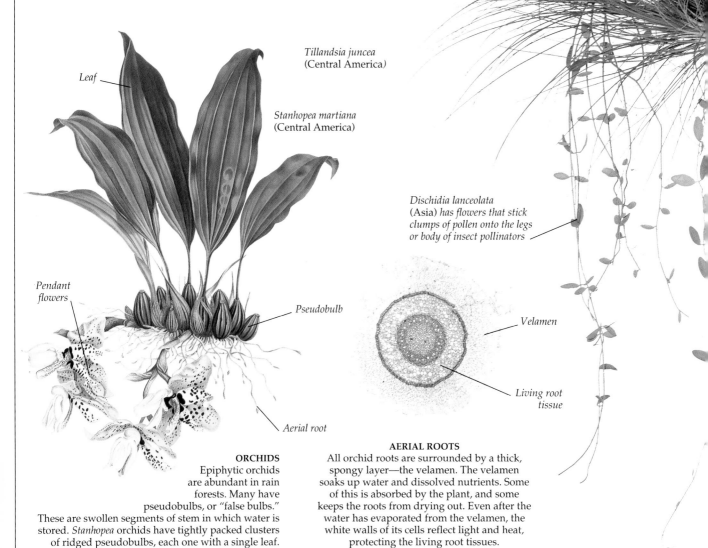

Leaf

Tillandsia juncea
(Central America)

Stanhopea martiana
(Central America)

Dischidia lanceolata
(Asia) *has flowers that stick clumps of pollen onto the legs or body of insect pollinators*

Pendant flowers

Pseudobulb

Velamen

Aerial root

Living root tissue

ORCHIDS
Epiphytic orchids are abundant in rain forests. Many have pseudobulbs, or "false bulbs." These are swollen segments of stem in which water is stored. *Stanhopea* orchids have tightly packed clusters of ridged pseudobulbs, each one with a single leaf.

AERIAL ROOTS
All orchid roots are surrounded by a thick, spongy layer—the velamen. The velamen soaks up water and dissolved nutrients. Some of this is absorbed by the plant, and some keeps the roots from drying out. Even after the water has evaporated from the velamen, the white walls of its cells reflect light and heat, protecting the living root tissues.

ium salviniae
ral America)

*This plant has leaves
at channel rain, dew, and
ris down to a mat of roots*

*This plant absorbs water
from the air through
scales on the leaves*

WATER TANKS
Epiphytic bromeliads, or urn plants, are found in New World rain forests. Each plant has a rosette of stiff leaves around a short stalk. The tightly overlapping leaf bases form a series of cups that collect rainwater. Plant fragments also become trapped, releasing nutrients into the water as they rot. Both water and dissolved minerals are absorbed by the bromeliad through specialized hairs on the leaf surface. These pools support an incredible number of aquatic insects and other creatures. Some frogs even breed in them.

Aechmea fasciata
(South America)

This plant has silver-veined leaves that have a velvety upper surface

Anthurium crystallinum
(South America)

Oncidium excavatum
(South America)

Tillandsia usneoides
(Central America)

*Young seedlings
like this have
anchoring roots;
the mature air
plants are a tangle
of stems and
narrow leaves*

Branching out

Heavy rain soon drains through the canopy, and the sunshine, though patchy, is very hot. This means that water and dissolved nutrients can be in short supply. Because of this, epiphytes share many of the characteristics of plants that grow in arid (hot and dry) conditions. The leaves have a thick, waxy, waterproof outer layer to reduce evaporation and grow so that rainwater funnels to the roots. The decomposing organic matter caught in water traps provides a source of fertilizer.

Guzmania lingulata
(Central America) *is a
bromeliad that prefers shade*

*Aechmea
purpurea-rosea*
(Brazil)

Climbers

ONE OF THE MOST impressive features of a tropical forest is the abundance of lianas, or climbing plants. Some lianas grow to a huge size, with long stems that climb to the forest canopy in search of light, looping from branch to branch and linking the crowns of trees. Once up in the canopy, they develop branches that bear leaves and flowers. Lianas send feeding roots—also called aerial roots because they dangle in midair—toward ground. When they reach soil, they bury themselves and branch rapidly. These long roots in turn act as supports for other climbing plants.

BLACK SPIDER MONKEY
Spider monkeys spend all their time in the trees, using their long limbs and tail to grip the branches.

Rhaphidophora decursiva

ROOT CLIMBERS
These climbers cling to a tree's bark with short clasping roots that come out at right angles from the nodes all along the stem. They either press into the crevices of rough bark or grow around a smooth surface. As the plant gets larger, feeding roots also sprout from the nodes. These roots go straight down to the ground.

Node

TENDRIL CLIMBERS
Vines like this *Teratostigma* send out straight tendrils that bend away from the light, sweeping slowly around until they come into contact with a stem or leaf. This contact causes the tendril to coil tightly and quickly—it wraps itself around a supporting stem within a few minutes.

Teratostigma (Southeast Asia)

Rhaphidophora decursiva (Southeast Asia)

Aerial root

Mesh

Fig

The fig sends aerial roots to the ground, where they spread through the soil

Roots grow branches that form a woody mesh around the trunk of the host

Fig kills the host tree by strangulation and by blocking out its light

STRANGLERS
Strangler figs destroy host trees when they grow. They begin life as epiphytes, and become very tall trees with hollow trunks.

Be serrati

GROWING TOGETHER
Strong climbing plants such as *Rhaphidophora decursiva* have juvenile leaves very different from the adult foliage. The young plants have short stems, with close overlapping "shingle" leaves that press against the bar to prevent loss of water. Later, long-stalked adult leave develop. In contrast, the climbing *Begonia serratipetala* is delicate, and its leaves shrivel if exposed to dry air.

Vine
Mondia whitei

REACHING THE TOP

...ain forest trees are draped
...he leafless stems and aerial
...of climbers. These need to
...ong but flexible, so that they
...t snap when the trees that
...ort them sway in high winds.

...rn
...rambling
...ward light
...er moss

TWINING PLANTS

These plants reach the light with
stems that twine around a support.
Once one stem is secured, others from
the same plant twine around it so that
a tough, twisted cord is made.

*Downward-
curving stamens*

Leptochilus decurrens
(Southeast Asia)

Young frond

*The internode,
or bare stem
between nodes,
gets longer as
the plant
grows*

Flower bud

CLIMBING FERNS

Ferns such as *Leptochilus decurrens* start life on the
damp, shady forest floor. The young fronds are
thin and delicate. The older ones are much tougher,
with a thick, waxy surface. These climbers reach
the light by scrambling over other vegetation.

Three-lobed leaf

...ASSIFLORA

...here are about 400
...ecies of *Passiflora* in
...opical jungles, most
...them in tropical
...merica. The young plant
...s short stems and no
...ndrils. It may stay this way
...r months on the shady
...rest floor. If a gap appears
...the canopy overhead, the
...lant begins to grow rapidly
...p toward the light.

Passiflora
(South America)

Central American jungles

ONCE THE CENTERS of the great Maya and Aztec civilizations, the small countries bridging North and South America contain an incredible diversity of plant and animal life. A large number of plants native to the region are found nowhere else, and it is home to many important tropical crops, including pawpaws, allspice, and vanilla. Central America and the Caribbean islands are particularly rich in bird life. The small country of Panama has more bird species than are found in the whole of North America, including migratory species that overwinter in the warm rain forests, before returning to North America to breed.

ANCIENT CULTURE
The Maya civilization flourished in Belize and Guatemala until A.D. 800. Mayans left many examples of intricately decorated pottery showing how they admired animals, such as this jaguar.

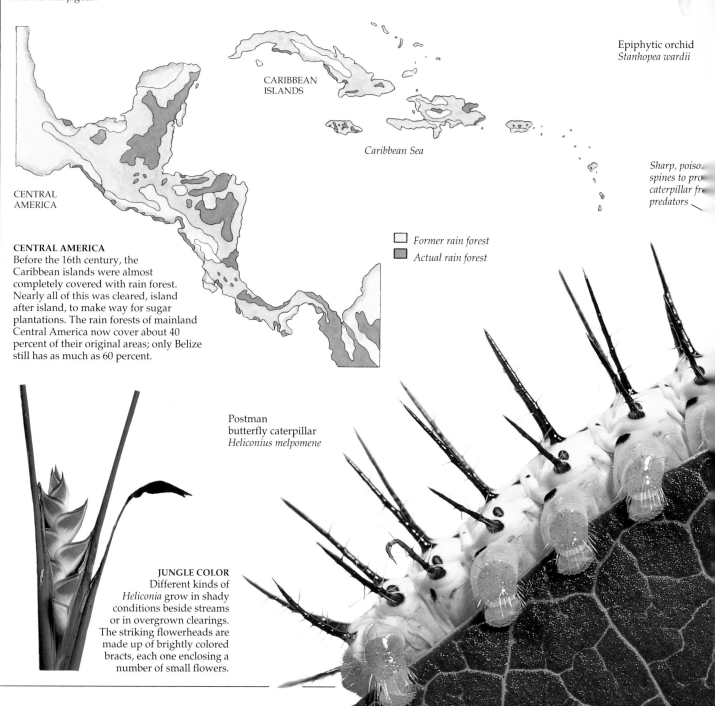

CARIBBEAN ISLANDS

Caribbean Sea

CENTRAL AMERICA

Epiphytic orchid
Stanhopea wardii

Sharp, poiso[...]
spines to pro[...]
caterpillar fr[...]
predators

☐ Former rain forest
▨ Actual rain forest

CENTRAL AMERICA
Before the 16th century, the Caribbean islands were almost completely covered with rain forest. Nearly all of this was cleared, island after island, to make way for sugar plantations. The rain forests of mainland Central America now cover about 40 percent of their original areas; only Belize still has as much as 60 percent.

Postman
butterfly caterpillar
Heliconius melpomene

JUNGLE COLOR
Different kinds of *Heliconia* grow in shady conditions beside streams or in overgrown clearings. The striking flowerheads are made up of brightly colored bracts, each one enclosing a number of small flowers.

WELL NOURISHED

These butterflies are able to live for six to nine months because they feed on protein-rich pollen as well as nectar. They squirt enzymes onto the pollen, which turns it into a "soup" that can be sucked up. Their longer lifespan means that they can lay more eggs.

Winged central column

Postman butterfly
Heliconius melpomene

BRIEF BEAUTY

Hanging in fragrant sprays, the large waxy flowers of this lowland epiphytic orchid are short-lived, withering after pollination. Each flower has a winged central column with fleshy lips, designed to attach the clumps of pollen firmly to its pollinator, the euglossine bee.

Scarlet macaw
Ara macao

WINGS IN THE TREETOPS

Raucous calls reveal the presence of these macaws in the treetops. These brightly colored, social birds squabble over nesting sites – tree holes at least 100 ft (30 m) above the ground. Their diet consists mostly of seeds, many of which are protected by a hard shell. The macaw uses its tongue to position a seed in the upper part of its beak, then cracks it with the lower part – just like a pair of pincers.

PROGRAMMED TO EAT

The postman butterfly caterpillar eats enormous numbers of leaves in the short time before it metamorphoses into a butterfly. Many postman butterfly caterpillars feed on *Passiflora* (passion flower) vines. For egg-laying purposes, the female butterfly always selects young shoots or tendrils that do not already have eggs on them, as the first caterpillars to hatch will devour any younger ones.

JUNGLE GOLD

The golden beetle *Plusiotis resplendens* is about 1 in (3 cm) long and is found only in Costa Rica. The adult beetles eat leaves, but the larvae feed on soft, rotting plants.

Slipper orchid
Paphiopedilum callosum
(Southeast Asia)

Sweet success

A FLOWER HAS TO BE POLLINATED before seeds ca develop. Flowers are made up of petals around th male (stamens) and female (carpels) reproductive parts that produce its seeds. During pollination, pollen is transferred from the stamens to the stign at the tip of a carpel. Pollination almost always ta place between plants of the same species, and stamens and carpels are often arranged so that self-pollination is not possible. Most jungle plants are pollinated by insects, birds, or ot small animals. In order to attract their pollinators, flowers offer sugary nectar protein-rich pollen as food. They draw attention to themselves with brightl colored petals or strong scents.

Line acting as nectar guide

Pouched petal

Short-t
leaf-nos
carrying
Anoura geo
(South Ame

EXOTIC ORCHID
Tropical slipper orchids are often pollinated by a single species of bee or hoverfly. The insect is guided to the center of the flower, where it is slippery, so it falls into a pouched petal. The only way out is to climb up hairs at the back of the pouch, a route that takes it past the stamens and pollen sacs.

BAT POLLINATION
Bat-pollinated flowers such as *Pachira aquatica* open at dusk, just as the bats are waking up. The bats are attracted to the flowers by a sour smell, and the flowers are arranged so that bats can reach them easily. As a bat drinks the nectar, its furry head is dusted with pollen from the long stamens, which it carries to the female stigma of the next flower.

Long stamens

NECTAR SIPPER
Bats that feed exclusively on nec have long tongues with a brushl tip, which quickly mops up poll as well as droplets of nectar. The bats can hover while feeding.

Shaving-brush tree
Pachira aquatica
(South America)

THE LONG AND THE SHORT OF IT
Most flowers are insect-pollinated. Short-tongued bees, flies, and beetles pollinate flat or cup-shaped flowers as they gather pollen and nectar. Only insects with longer tongues can reach nectar hidden in tubular flowers. This flowering shrub (*Steriphoma pardoxum*) has long stamens that ripen before the stigma, in order to prevent self-pollination. It is pollinated by long-tongued insects such as hawkmoths.

Orchid bee
Euglossa assarophora
(South America)

EUGLOSSINE BEES
Male euglossine bees, known as orchid bees, pollinate orchids when they visit them, scraping aromatic (strong-smelling) substances from parts of the flower. Females forage over a large area, pollinating a wide variety of plants at all levels of the forest.

Orchid bee
Euglossa intersecta
(South America)

Scarlet-chested
sunbird
*Nectarinia
senegalensis*
(Africa)

PARALLEL EVOLUTION
Sunbirds are the Old World equivalents of the hummingbirds of the Western Hemisphere. Like them, they feed on nectar from flowers, and they eat many insects as well. But sunbirds do not hover – they perch beside the flowers.

*Steriphoma
pardoxum*
(South America)

Wings flap at least
90 times per second

Brown violet-ear
Colibri delphinea
(Central America)

QUICK AS A FLASH
Hummingbirds hover in front of flowers, their wings making a figure-eight movement, which allows them to maneuver easily. Bird-pollinated flowers are usually red or bright orange. Nectar, though sweet and sugary, is low in protein content, so nectar-eating birds need a constant supply of flowers to get enough to eat. The pollen eaten with the nectar is a valuable source of protein.

Hummingbird sucks
up nectar with the long
tongue inside its beak

Hotlips
Cephaelis elata
(Central America)

Seed dispersal

P<small>LANTS</small> N<small>EED</small> to spread their seeds so that they have room to grow. Because they cannot move around, they rely on wind, animals, water, or explosive pods to scatter their seeds. The fruit wall is part of this scattering mechanism. Some fruits are winged or cottony to help the seeds become airborne. Some are air-filled and float on water. More familiar are the juicy, brightly colored fruits that spread their seeds by enticing animals, including people, to eat their succulent flesh. These seeds are spread when animals spit them out, let them fall, or pass them out in droppings deposited some distance away.

HEALTHY APPETITE
The great Indian hornbill (*Buceros bicornis*) is an avid fruit eater. Seeds germinate from its droppings.

Hard seed case

ATTRACTIVE MORSEL
This *Elaeocarpus angustifolia* seed was enclosed in a purple fruit with oily flesh. The fruit is swallowed whole by birds, such as hornbills.

BURIED AND FORGOTTEN
Inside the fibrous case of *Loxococcus rupicola* is a hard nutty seed that is dispersed by rodents. These gnawing animals bury seeds for future feasts. Forgotten caches germinate and grow.

RATTAN PALMS
Rattan palms produce clusters of fruits. These usually contain a single seed enveloped in a fleshy layer that is eaten by birds and animals. As hard-shelled seeds pass through the digestive tract of an animal, their outer wall is eaten away by digestive juices. This makes water absorption and germination easier.

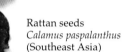

Fruit is clusters base of f

Rattan seeds
Calamus paspalanthus
(Southeast Asia)

Red lemur palm fr
Lemurophoenix halleuxii
(Madagascar)

A CASE THAT IS HARD TO CRACK?
Larger animals and fruit-eating bats often carry fruit to a safe place before eating it. Some seeds are then spat out or discarded, especially if they are too hard to crack.

Pigafetta filaris
(Australasia)

Ha nutty s

FRUIT EATER
This lemur lives in tall trees beside rivers in southern Madagascar. Fruit is the most important part of its diet, although it also eats insects and leaves.

Ring-tailed lemur
Lemur catta
(Madagascar)

Sago palm
Metroxylon sagu
(Australasia)

SCALY FRU
Pigafetta, sag and rattan paln are closely relat species with fru enclosed in shin overlapping scale Beneath a sago palm scales is a corky layer th enables the fruit to float, th dispersing its single seed. sago palm dies after it has fruite

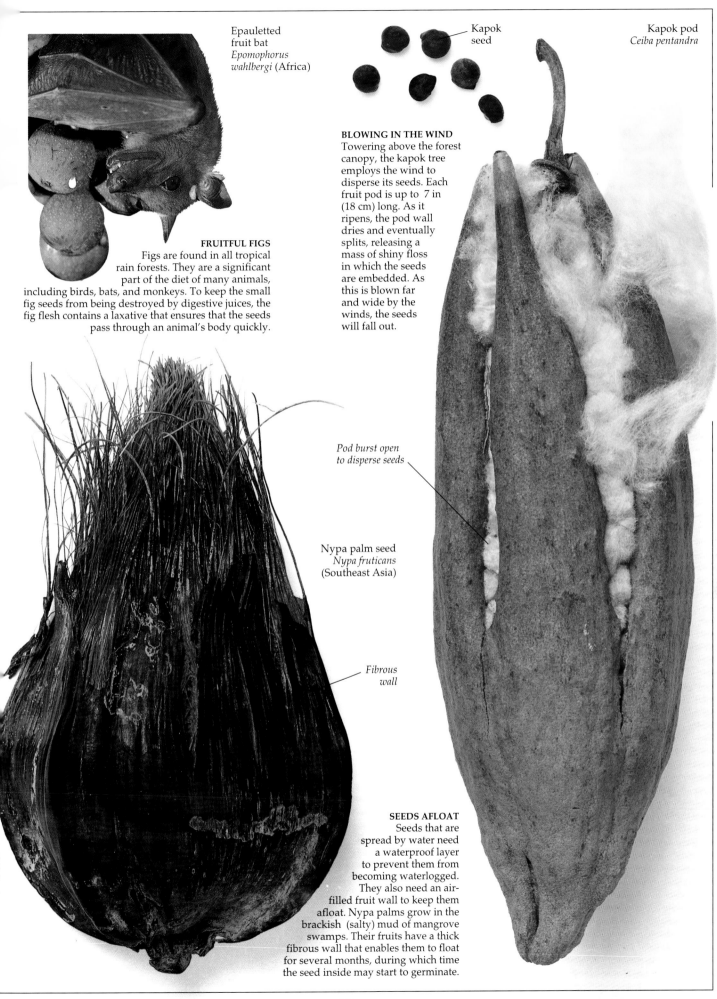

Epauletted
fruit bat
*Epomophorus
wahlbergi* (Africa)

Kapok
seed

Kapok pod
Ceiba pentandra

BLOWING IN THE WIND
Towering above the forest
canopy, the kapok tree
employs the wind to
disperse its seeds. Each
fruit pod is up to 7 in
(18 cm) long. As it
ripens, the pod wall
dries and eventually
splits, releasing a
mass of shiny floss
in which the seeds
are embedded. As
this is blown far
and wide by the
winds, the seeds
will fall out.

FRUITFUL FIGS
Figs are found in all tropical
rain forests. They are a significant
part of the diet of many animals,
including birds, bats, and monkeys. To keep the small
fig seeds from being destroyed by digestive juices, the
fig flesh contains a laxative that ensures that the seeds
pass through an animal's body quickly.

*Pod burst open
to disperse seeds*

Nypa palm seed
Nypa fruticans
(Southeast Asia)

*Fibrous
wall*

SEEDS AFLOAT
Seeds that are
spread by water need
a waterproof layer
to prevent them from
becoming waterlogged.
They also need an air-
filled fruit wall to keep them
afloat. Nypa palms grow in the
brackish (salty) mud of mangrove
swamps. Their fruits have a thick
fibrous wall that enables them to float
for several months, during which time
the seed inside may start to germinate.

Dusk to dawn

NIGHT COMES SWIFTLY in the tropics, wh●
there are no lingering hours of twilight. A●
the sun sinks toward the horizon, daytim●
creatures return to their roosts or nests, a●
new group of animals awakens. Because
some animals are active by day and other●
night, different species of animals that wo●
otherwise compete for food and space are
separated. The cooler night air brings out
insects and amphibians with thin, moist
skins, and small mammals that hunt on th●
forest floor. Nocturnal (nighttime) animal●
are specially adapted—many have huge e●
or acutely sensitive ears and noses. Yet the
jungle is never completely dark. The moo●
shines on clear nights. Fireflies flash throu●
the trees, and phosphorescent fungi glow
eerily on the forest floor, until they are
devoured by beetles.

NIGHT FEEDER
By day, Franquet's epauleted
bats roost in small groups, hanging
from thin branches usually 13-20 ft
(4-6 m) above the ground. As
night falls, they fly off to feed on
fruit, large numbers often gathering
in a heavily laden tree. Fruit bats
have large eyes with good vision,
but they locate ripe fruit with
their keen sense of smell.

Franquet's epauleted bat
Epomops franqueti
(Africa)

*Wings folded
when roosting*

FLYING HOME TO ROOST
Just before darkness falls, parties
of toucans fly off to roost in
selected trees. They look ungainly
in flight, but although large, their
colorful bills are very light in
weight. As dawn breaks, the
flock once more takes to the
air in search of ripe fruit.

*Large curved
beak for picking
and eating fruit*

Cuvier's toucan
Rhamphastos cuvieri
(South America)

NIGHT-LIGHTS
Fireflies are not the only insects that
glow. Males of this species of click
beetle, *Pyrophorus*, from tropical
America, fly among the trees flashing
in special sequences that are answered
only by females of the same species.

NECTAR-SIPPERS

Night-flying moths feed on the nectar of sweetly scented, pale-colored flowers, many of which are open only for a single night. This African moon moth is one of the largest species, with a wingspan of 5 in (12 cm). The feathery antennae of the male are so sensitive that they can pick up the slightest trace of pheromones (sex hormones) wafting from a female moth.

African moon moth
Argema mimosae
(Africa)

BIG EYES

The vertical pupils of the red-eyed tree frog *Agalychnis callidryas* open up at night to help it see in the very low light levels. By day, the pupils become slits. These frogs live and feed up in the canopy. Only the female comes down to absorb water from a stream before she lays her eggs.

DAWN CHORUS

Just before dawn breaks, howler monkeys set up a noisy chorus. The deafening howls can be heard up to 2 miles (3 km) away, and are produced by air passing over the hyoid bone in the large larynx. Mature males, such as this one, make the loudest howl. The howl can be amplified by their body position. This early morning symphony is a warning to other groups of howlers not to come too close to them and their food supply.

Large eyes for night vision

Red howler monkey
Alouatta seniculus
(South America)

GHT MONKEY

e douroucouli, or
ght monkey, is the only
cturnal monkey in the
rld. As night falls,
ouroucoulis emerge from
e holes to feed on fruit,
aves, insects, and other
all animals. Their large,
rward-pointing eyes are
pical of nocturnal
imates, and help them
see in the near-darkness
they climb and leap
om branch to branch.

Douroucouli
Aotus trivirgatus
(South America)

DIGGING DOWN

The scaly Indian pangolin, *Manis crassicaudata*, digs a burrow in which it spends the day, emerging at night to forage on the forest floor. Though its sight is weak, it has an acute sense of smell, which it uses to locate ant and termite mounds. Breaking in with the long powerful claws on its forelimbs, the pangolin flicks its very long sticky tongue into chambers full of insects, eggs, and pupae. It is toothless, so the swallowed insects are ground up in the lower part of its stomach.

South American jungles

THE AMAZON BASIN covers a vast area, 2.3 million sq. mil
(6 million sq. km), and is covered by the world's largest
expanse of tropical rain forest. This jungle supports more
species of plants and animals than anywhere else – about
one fifth of the world's bird and flowering plant species, a
about one tenth of all mammal species. No definite figure
can be put on the number of different insects because man
have yet to be identified – or even discovered – by scientis
Amerindian tribes have lived in these forests for about
12,000 years, during which time they have built up a detai
and valuable knowledge of the jungle's plants, many of
which they use in their
everyday lives.

Mouth of Amazon River

SOUTH AMERICA

☐ *Former rain forest*
▨ *Actual rain forest*

SOUTH AMERICA
The forests of the northwest
were separated from
the Amazonian forests
2 million years ago by the
formation of the Andes
Mountains. A few small
patches are all that remain
of the once continuous
strip of forest along the
Atlantic coast of Brazil.

BODY PAINTING
These Yanomamo girls
belong to one of 143
tribal groups remaining
in Amazonia. Body
painting is popular, with
paint from plants such
as urucu or achiote.
The seeds are wiped
directly onto the skin
or boiled to make a
paste. Each tribe has
its favorite patterns.

Aphinte
Bixa orellana

A WAXY SURFACE
Growing naturally beside rivers and around the edges
of swampy areas, the Brazilian wax palm, *Copernicia
prunifera*, is also cultivated in Brazil for the carnauba
wax that covers the surface of its leaves. Carnauba is a
top quality wax with a high melting point of 161°F
(70°C). It is used chiefly in the cosmetic and polish
industries. The wax flakes off leaves that have been
picked and dried in the sun. Wax taken from the
young leaves is known as "prime yellow," and about
1,300 leaves are needed to obtain 2.2 lbs (1 kg) of wax.

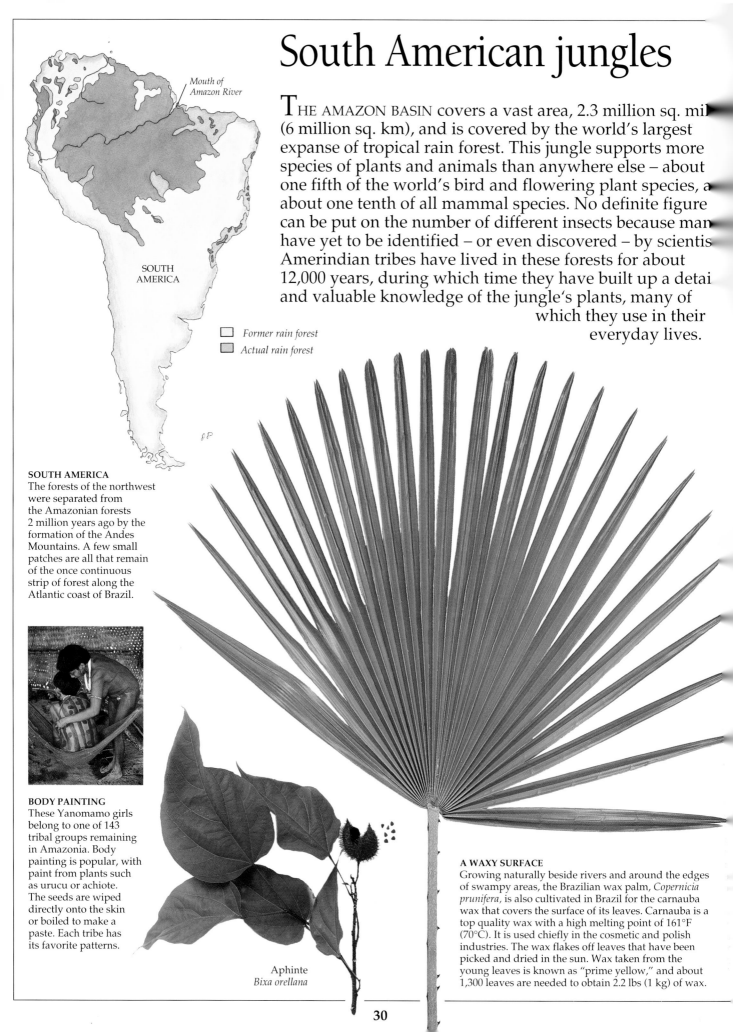

ONE OF MANY
The malachite butterfly
is just one of more than
2,000 species of butterfly
in the Amazonian jungles.
They fly during the day,
pausing to feed on over-
ripe fruit fermenting on
the forest floor.

Malachite butterfly
Metamorpha stelenes

GOLD IN THE FOREST
This beautiful golden monkey is found only
in Atlantic coastal rain forests. Golden lion
tamarins live in mature forest, where they
forage for invertebrates, small animals, and fruit
10-30 ft (3-10 m) up in the liana-covered trees.
They came near to extinction in the 1960s,
because their habitat was being destroyed and
hundreds were being exported as pets every
year. Since then, captive breeding programs
established in the United States and Europe
have resulted in the release of golden lion
tamarins back into the wild.

Long tail for balancing

en lion tamarin
opithecus rosalia

Buriti palm
Mauritia flexuosa

E TREE OF LIFE
thing of this tall palm goes to
ste. The Amerindians use it
a source of food, fibers, wood,
k, and thatching. Wine made
m its vitamin C-rich fruits is
en to the elderly and sick.

T SO LAZY
spite its name, the
ree-toed sloth
dypus tridactylus is
t a lazy animal. It is
rfectly adapted to its
e up in the canopy.
ere is little protein in
diet, and to conserve
ergy it hangs upside
own and its strong
aws lock so tightly
to branches that it
oes not fall off even
hen asleep – or dead!

Amazon lily
Eucharis amazonica

MYSTERIOUS POWERS
The Amazon lily grows
on the lower slopes of the
Andes. The Kofan tribes
of western Colombia and
northern Ecuador boil the
whole plant, including its
bulb, to make a tea. This
tea is drunk by men
before they hunt
monkeys, in the belief
that it will make them
more accurate
with the blowpipe.

Beside the water

THE RIVERBANK IS THE DOMAIN of animals that live both on land and in water. The vegetation is particularly dense, as the open expanse of water allows extra light to reach the ground. This mosaic of water, overhanging branches, and tangle of waterside ferns, sedges, and saplings provides an ideal environment for animals that live and breed on land, but enter the water to hunt and feed. However, heavy rains sometimes cause a riverbank to burst, which puts at risk those animals nesting close to the water's edge.

JAWS OF THE RIVERBANK
The saltwater crocodile, *Croco porosus*, is the world's large crocodile. It can reach 25 ft (7.5 length and weigh as much as 3

UMBRELLA GRASS
The sedge, *Cyperus alternifolia*, has leaves that radiate from the top of its tall stems like the spokes of an umbrella. Underwater, the roots grow into an impenetrable tangle that helps stabilize the edges of swamps in which it grows.

WARY WATER LIZARD
Water dragons are agamid lizards that live beside water in the forests of Southeast Asia and Australia. Although they are mainly tree dwellers, they can run quickly over the ground on their two hind legs. When not searching for invertebrates, eggs, or nestlings to eat, they spend most of their time resting on a branch hanging over the water. They are extremely wary and, at the slightest disturbance, will drop off into the water, which may be as much as 30 ft (9 m) below.

Crested water dragon
Physignathus sp.
(Asia)

WATERSIDE PLANT
The waterside plant *Thalia geniculata* is abundant in marshes and seasonally flooded ground near rivers. It has large waxy leaves and spreads by means of tuberous roots.

An alert crested water dragon stands on all four feet, watching for danger

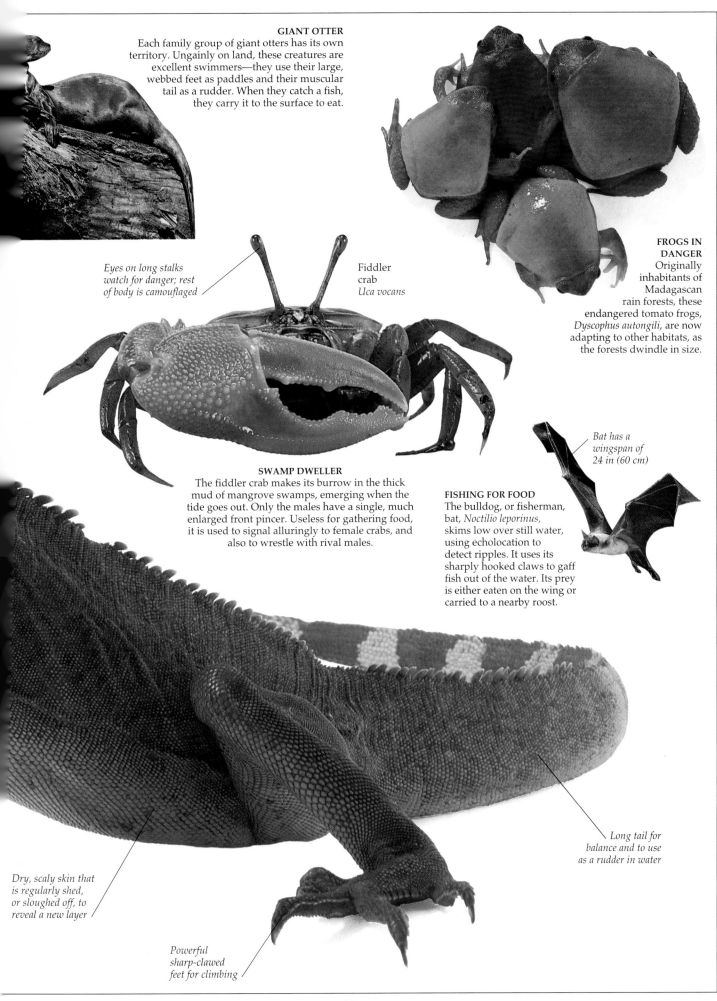

GIANT OTTER
Each family group of giant otters has its own territory. Ungainly on land, these creatures are excellent swimmers—they use their large, webbed feet as paddles and their muscular tail as a rudder. When they catch a fish, they carry it to the surface to eat.

FROGS IN DANGER
Originally inhabitants of Madagascan rain forests, these endangered tomato frogs, *Dyscophus autongili*, are now adapting to other habitats, as the forests dwindle in size.

Eyes on long stalks watch for danger; rest of body is camouflaged

Fiddler crab
Uca vocans

SWAMP DWELLER
The fiddler crab makes its burrow in the thick mud of mangrove swamps, emerging when the tide goes out. Only the males have a single, much enlarged front pincer. Useless for gathering food, it is used to signal alluringly to female crabs, and also to wrestle with rival males.

Bat has a wingspan of 24 in (60 cm)

FISHING FOR FOOD
The bulldog, or fisherman, bat, *Noctilio leporinus*, skims low over still water, using echolocation to detect ripples. It uses its sharply hooked claws to gaff fish out of the water. Its prey is either eaten on the wing or carried to a nearby roost.

Long tail for balance and to use as a rudder in water

Dry, scaly skin that is regularly shed, or sloughed off, to reveal a new layer

Powerful sharp-clawed feet for climbing

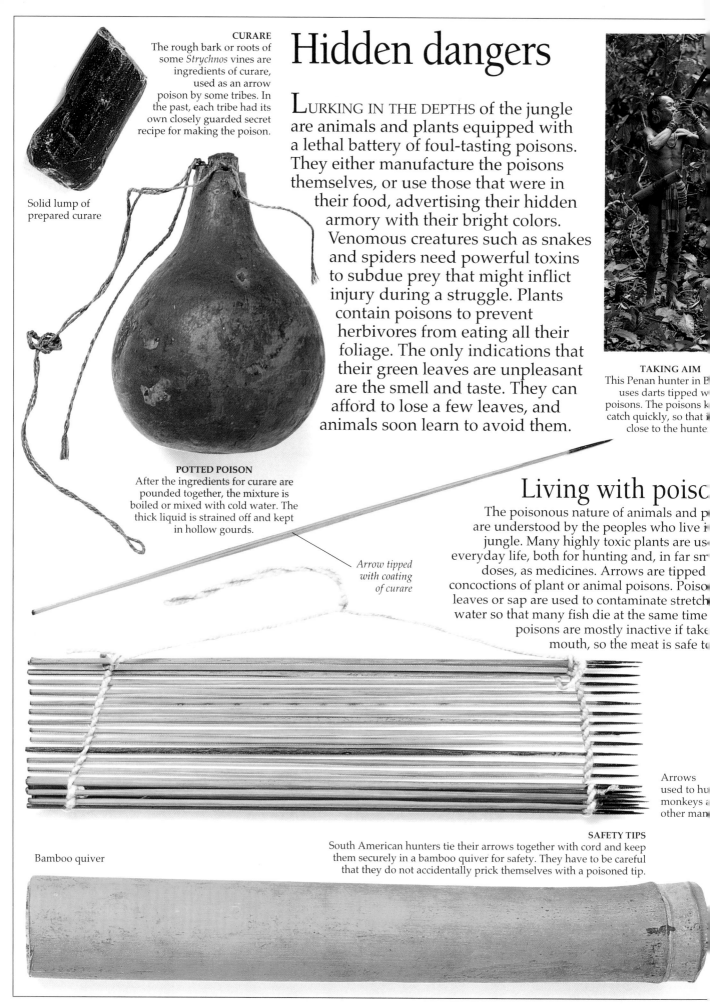

CURARE
The rough bark or roots of some *Strychnos* vines are ingredients of curare, used as an arrow poison by some tribes. In the past, each tribe had its own closely guarded secret recipe for making the poison.

Solid lump of prepared curare

Hidden dangers

LURKING IN THE DEPTHS of the jungle are animals and plants equipped with a lethal battery of foul-tasting poisons. They either manufacture the poisons themselves, or use those that were in their food, advertising their hidden armory with their bright colors. Venomous creatures such as snakes and spiders need powerful toxins to subdue prey that might inflict injury during a struggle. Plants contain poisons to prevent herbivores from eating all their foliage. The only indications that their green leaves are unpleasant are the smell and taste. They can afford to lose a few leaves, and animals soon learn to avoid them.

TAKING AIM
This Penan hunter in B
uses darts tipped w
poisons. The poisons k
catch quickly, so that
close to the hunte

POTTED POISON
After the ingredients for curare are pounded together, the mixture is boiled or mixed with cold water. The thick liquid is strained off and kept in hollow gourds.

Arrow tipped with coating of curare

Living with poiso

The poisonous nature of animals and p
are understood by the peoples who live i
jungle. Many highly toxic plants are us
everyday life, both for hunting and, in far sm
doses, as medicines. Arrows are tipped
concoctions of plant or animal poisons. Poiso
leaves or sap are used to contaminate stretch
water so that many fish die at the same time
poisons are mostly inactive if take
mouth, so the meat is safe t

Arrows
used to hu
monkeys
other man

SAFETY TIPS
South American hunters tie their arrows together with cord and keep them securely in a bamboo quiver for safety. They have to be careful that they do not accidentally prick themselves with a poisoned tip.

Bamboo quiver

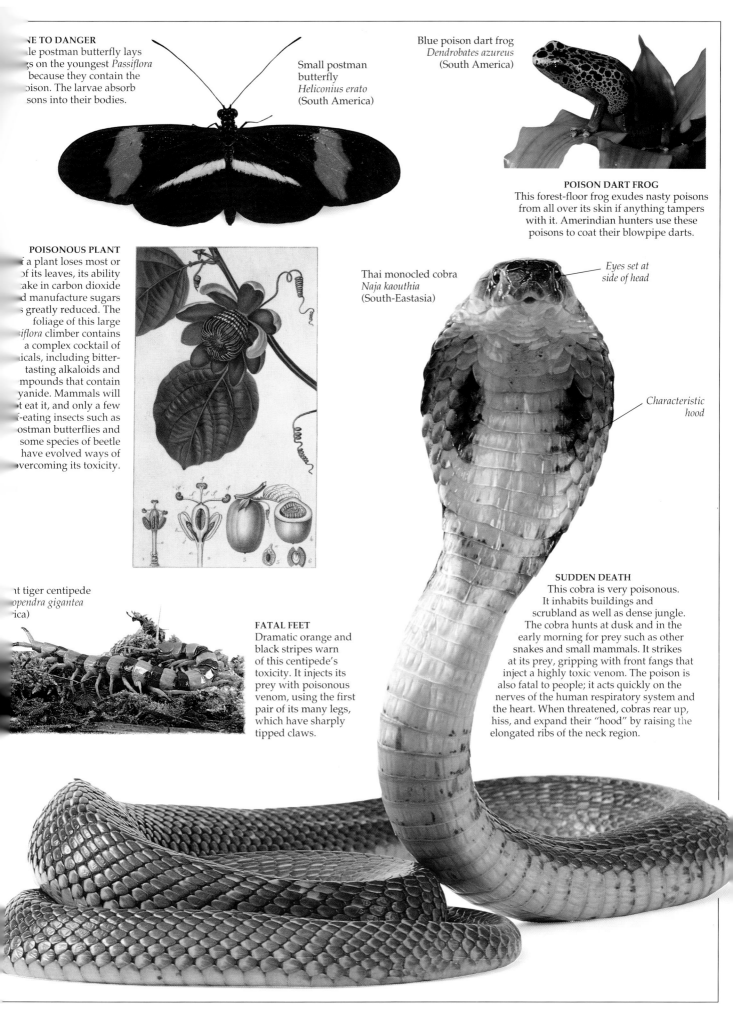

le postman butterfly lays
gs on the youngest *Passiflora*
because they contain the
oison. The larvae absorb
sons into their bodies.

Small postman
butterfly
Heliconius erato
(South America)

Blue poison dart frog
Dendrobates azureus
(South America)

POISON DART FROG

This forest-floor frog exudes nasty poisons
from all over its skin if anything tampers
with it. Amerindian hunters use these
poisons to coat their blowpipe darts.

POISONOUS PLANT

f a plant loses most or
of its leaves, its ability
ake in carbon dioxide
d manufacture sugars
greatly reduced. The
foliage of this large
iflora climber contains
a complex cocktail of
icals, including bitter-
tasting alkaloids and
mpounds that contain
yanide. Mammals will
t eat it, and only a few
-eating insects such as
ostman butterflies and
some species of beetle
have evolved ways of
vercoming its toxicity.

Thai monocled cobra
Naja kaouthia
(South-Eastasia)

*Eyes set at
side of head*

*Characteristic
hood*

t tiger centipede
opendra gigantea
ica)

FATAL FEET

Dramatic orange and
black stripes warn
of this centipede's
toxicity. It injects its
prey with poisonous
venom, using the first
pair of its many legs,
which have sharply
tipped claws.

SUDDEN DEATH

This cobra is very poisonous.
It inhabits buildings and
scrubland as well as dense jungle.
The cobra hunts at dusk and in the
early morning for prey such as other
snakes and small mammals. It strikes
at its prey, gripping with front fangs that
inject a highly toxic venom. The poison is
also fatal to people; it acts quickly on the
nerves of the human respiratory system and
the heart. When threatened, cobras rear up,
hiss, and expand their "hood" by raising the
elongated ribs of the neck region.

Nature's architects

THE RAIN FOREST PROVIDES tree holes, tangles of lianas, and plenty of other hideaways. In spite of this, numerous creatures build custom-made homes from forest materials. Social insects such as bees, wasps, ants, and termites construct elaborate nests inside of which a teeming mass of insects live and tend their larvae. These large colonies need well-protected structures to keep predators out. Some structures last for years. Birds are master weavers, but their nests are used only to rear young. Even less permanent are the beds made by gorillas. Every night, they prepare a mattress of leaves on the ground or among low branches.

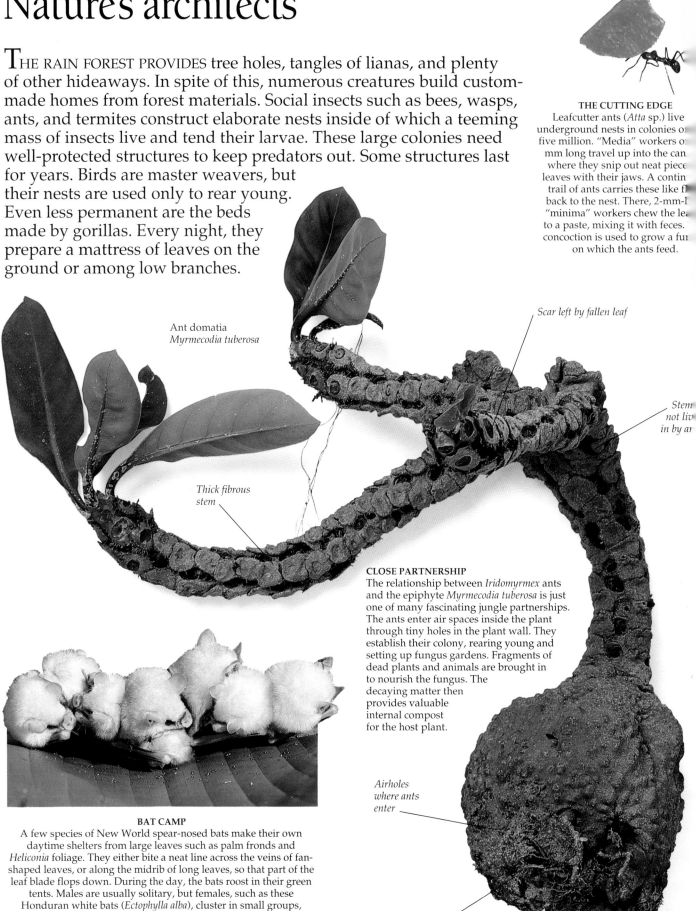

THE CUTTING EDGE
Leafcutter ants (*Atta* sp.) live underground nests in colonies of five million. "Media" workers of mm long travel up into the can where they snip out neat piece leaves with their jaws. A contin trail of ants carries these like fl back to the nest. There, 2-mm-l "minima" workers chew the lea to a paste, mixing it with feces. concoction is used to grow a fur on which the ants feed.

Scar left by fallen leaf

Ant domatia
Myrmecodia tuberosa

Stem
not liv
in by ar

Thick fibrous
stem

CLOSE PARTNERSHIP
The relationship between *Iridomyrmex* ants and the epiphyte *Myrmecodia tuberosa* is just one of many fascinating jungle partnerships. The ants enter air spaces inside the plant through tiny holes in the plant wall. They establish their colony, rearing young and setting up fungus gardens. Fragments of dead plants and animals are brought in to nourish the fungus. The decaying matter then provides valuable internal compost for the host plant.

Airholes
where ants
enter

BAT CAMP
A few species of New World spear-nosed bats make their own daytime shelters from large leaves such as palm fronds and *Heliconia* foliage. They either bite a neat line across the veins of fan-shaped leaves, or along the midrib of long leaves, so that part of the leaf blade flops down. During the day, the bats roost in their green tents. Males are usually solitary, but females, such as these Honduran white bats (*Ectophylla alba*), cluster in small groups, especially while rearing their young.

Swollen
base of plant

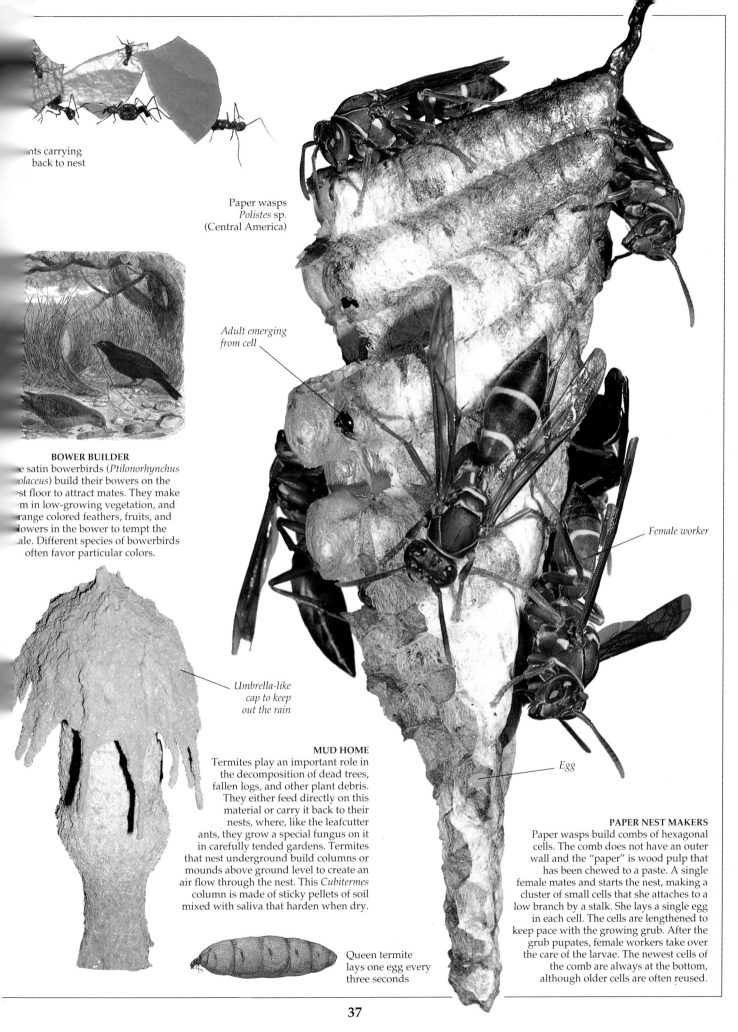

...nts carrying
...back to nest

Paper wasps
Polistes sp.
(Central America)

*Adult emerging
from cell*

Female worker

Egg

BOWER BUILDER
...e satin bowerbirds (*Ptilonorhynchus
...olaceus*) build their bowers on the
...st floor to attract mates. They make
...m in low-growing vegetation, and
...range colored feathers, fruits, and
...owers in the bower to tempt the
...ale. Different species of bowerbirds
often favor particular colors.

*Umbrella-like
cap to keep
out the rain*

MUD HOME
Termites play an important role in
the decomposition of dead trees,
fallen logs, and other plant debris.
They either feed directly on this
material or carry it back to their
nests, where, like the leafcutter
ants, they grow a special fungus on it
in carefully tended gardens. Termites
that nest underground build columns or
mounds above ground level to create an
air flow through the nest. This *Cubitermes*
column is made of sticky pellets of soil
mixed with saliva that harden when dry.

*Queen termite
lays one egg every
three seconds*

PAPER NEST MAKERS
Paper wasps build combs of hexagonal
cells. The comb does not have an outer
wall and the "paper" is wood pulp that
has been chewed to a paste. A single
female mates and starts the nest, making a
cluster of small cells that she attaches to a
low branch by a stalk. She lays a single egg
in each cell. The cells are lengthened to
keep pace with the growing grub. After the
grub pupates, female workers take over
the care of the larvae. The newest cells of
the comb are always at the bottom,
although older cells are often reused.

Tribes make their hunting weapons from rain forest materials. This spear from Guyana is made from feathers, wood, bone, and basketry. The palmwood bow is strung with rattan, and the three-tipped fish arrow is made of wood, bamboo, reed, and cane.

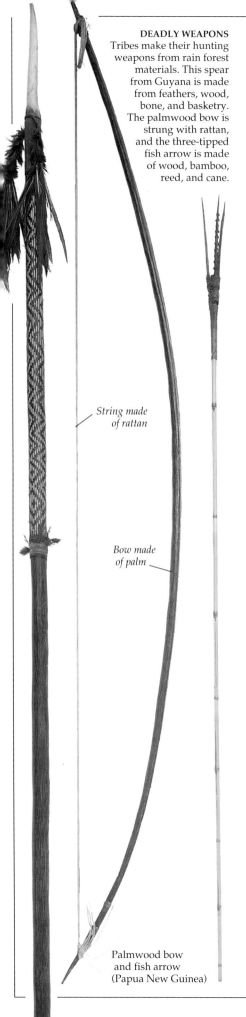

String made of rattan

Bow made of palm

Palmwood bow and fish arrow (Papua New Guinea)

House and home

WHEN PEOPLE NEED shelter, there is no shortage of building materials in the jungle. Slender tree trunks are felled for use as walls; palm fronds are cut for thatching; and tough cording is prepared from lianas. Some tribes build separate family homes grouped together in a forest clearing. Others favor one enormous structure that houses the whole community, and inside of which each family has its own hearth. Styles vary, but the houses share some features, such as an overhanging thatched roof to keep out the rain. Inside, each dwelling contains everyday utensils and weapons, skillfully made from natural materials such as bamboo and cane.

POTTER'S ART
The neolithic Kintampo culture bro_____ pottery to the African rain fores_____ Containers such as this partly glaze_____ from lower Zaire are still made to_____

Model of a rain forest house without walls (South America)

Sturdy tree trunks form basic structure

WELL SHIELDED
Warring tribespeople held shields to ward off blows from spears or arrows. Today, they are more often used for ceremonial purposes. This colorful shield from Borneo is decorated on the front with human hair. The reverse depicts tigers and dragons, symbols of strength and invincibility.

Human hairs

Dyak shield (Borneo)

HIGH AND DRY
This hill tribe house in northern Thailand has central living quarters. It is well screened from the rain by thatching that sweeps down on all sides. The house is set on poles above the ground to keep the floor dry. Outside, there is plenty of shelter beneath the roof for outdoor tasks.

NATIVE HOUSE AT DORERI
Traveling by water is the easiest way to get around much of New Guinea because of the dense jungle vegetation. Many settlements are therefore built on the riverside or by the coast. This large house has been built on stilts over the water, probably in order to escape destructive insects such as termites.

LIVING IN THE RAIN FOREST
This model gives some idea of the the furniture and utensils found in a native rain forest house in South America. The occupants sleep in hammocks, knotted from cords. They weave lightweight vessels from cane or palm leaves, but heavy duty containers are made with strips of wood. Canoe paddles and weapons are also shaped from wood, and all of these items are stored by hanging them on the walls of the house. Clay pots are not made by all tribes, but are often acquired by trading.

Hammock

Fishing basket

CHIEF'S YAM HOUSE
Yams are an important staple food. On the Trobriand Islands, off the coast of New Guinea, yams are also a central part of complicated rituals that maintain goodwill and kinship between clans related by marriage. After the yam harvest, the chief's yam house is filled first. This brightly decorated house is thatched and has well-ventilated walls. This allows air to circulate so that the yams do not get moldy.

African jungles

ALTHOUGH THEY CONTAIN an impressive 17,000 species of flowering plants, African rain forests have fewer species than those of either America or Asia. There are also fewer kinds of ferns. This is because the climate of Africa became much drier during the last ice age, which ended about 12,000 years ago. Many animals, insects, and plants died out during this period. Those that survived lived in three well-separated pockets of forest that remained moist. As the ice retreated from the lands farther north, the climate became wetter, and the surviving rain forest species spread out from their isolated refuges.

OIL PALM
This 33-65 ft (10-20 m) palm (*Elaeis guineensis*) yields two valuable oils – palm oil from the red fibrous fruit pulp and palm kernel oil from the seeds.

STICKY FEET
The Madagascan day gecko (*Phe... madagascariensis*) has Velcro-like pads so it can cling to branches – even run along their underside.

☐ *Former rain fores...*
☐ *Actual rain forest*

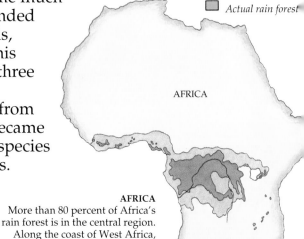

AFRICA

AFRICA
More than 80 percent of Africa's rain forest is in the central region. Along the coast of West Africa, the remaining forests are in fragmented pockets, but some countries are setting up conservation zones.

Madag...

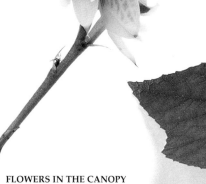

FLOWERS IN THE CANOPY
Of all the epiphytic flowering plants and ferns that grow in African jungles, over 60% are different kinds of orchids, and little is known about their life histories. *Polystachya galeata* comes from Sierra Leone, where new reserves will help to safeguard its future and that of other vulnerable species.

FAST GROWTH
Hibiscus shrubs grow quickly, up to 7 ft (2 m) tall. They flourish along the edges of the forest, where there is the most light. Their large flowers attract pollinators such as bees and butterflies.

Hibiscus
Hibiscus calyphyllus

GOOD APPETITES
African elephants prefer to browse the dense vegetation of clearings and forest margins. Over half of their diet is foliage from trees and large climbers, but they will travel far into the depths of the jungle to find their favorite tree fruits.

Black-and-white colobus
Colobus guereza
(Africa)

Senegal parrot
Poicephalus senegalensis
(Africa)

FLASH OF COLOR
The green and gold Senegal parrots migrate across savanna grassland into the forest to take advantage of ripening crops of fruits and seeds. They nest in unlined tree holes.

FAMILY GROUP
The guereza is one of four kinds of black-and-white colobus monkey that live in family groups in the treetops. It is found in central and eastern Africa. Because these monkeys eat a wide range of readily available leaves, they do not need a very large home range.

Only males have a silver back

arge, werful nds

HEAD OF THE TRIBE
This silverback lowland gorilla *(Gorilla gorilla gorilla)* is a mature male. He is the dominant head of a social group that also contains mature females and young gorillas. Silverbacks are gentle with their young, but as the males reach maturity, they have to leave the troop and form their own social group. Gorillas travel slowly through the forest, resting, playing, and eating leaves, stems, and shoots.

Wing-stalked
yam powder

Medicines

Wing-stalked yam
Dioscorea alata
(Southeast Asia)

MOST OF THESE PLANTS are very poisonous. Yet, if taken at the right dosage, they help save lives or alleviate suffering. A rain forest can be compared to a giant pharmacy where tribespeople find remedies for all their ills. Only some of the medicinal plants have been screened scientifically. It is important to do this either before the plants become extinct, or the tribes, with their accumulated knowledge, disappear. Many plants are known to contain beneficial compounds. Others have a more spiritual importance. Some tribespeople think if a plant looks like a bodily organ, it will cure that organ of all ailments.

SKIN MEDICINE
Chaulmoogra ointment is an I
preparation rubbed onto the s
treat leprosy and skin infecti

Seed or
used in
chauln
ointme

Hydnocarpus fruit and seed
Hydnocarpus kurzii
(Southeast Asia)

INDIAN YAM
Yams are a good source of diosgenin, a compound used in oral contraceptives. It is also used in treatments for rheumatoid arthritis and rheumatic fever.

Red cinchona bark
Cinchona succirubra
(South America)

Dried tongue of
pirarucu fish
(South America)

Guarana bark
Paullinia cupana
(South America)

*Quinine stored
in the bark*

HARD MEDICINE
This hard fruit comes from the *Hydnoc*
tree, grown in Burma, Thailand, ar
India for its medicinal properties

Heckel chew
Garcinia kola
(Africa)

PRECIOUS PLANT
The red cinchona tree is one of four commercial kinds of *Cinchona*. The quinine extracted from the bark and roots is an important part of the treatment of malaria, although synthetic drugs are also available today.

STIMULATING DRINKS
Guarana plants contain caffeine and are made into tonic drinks all over South America. Tribes grate the seeds (above) or bark into water with the rough, dried tongue of the pirarucu fish. Strong bitter doses are used to get rid of intestinal worms. The seeds are used commercially in carbonated drinks.

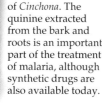

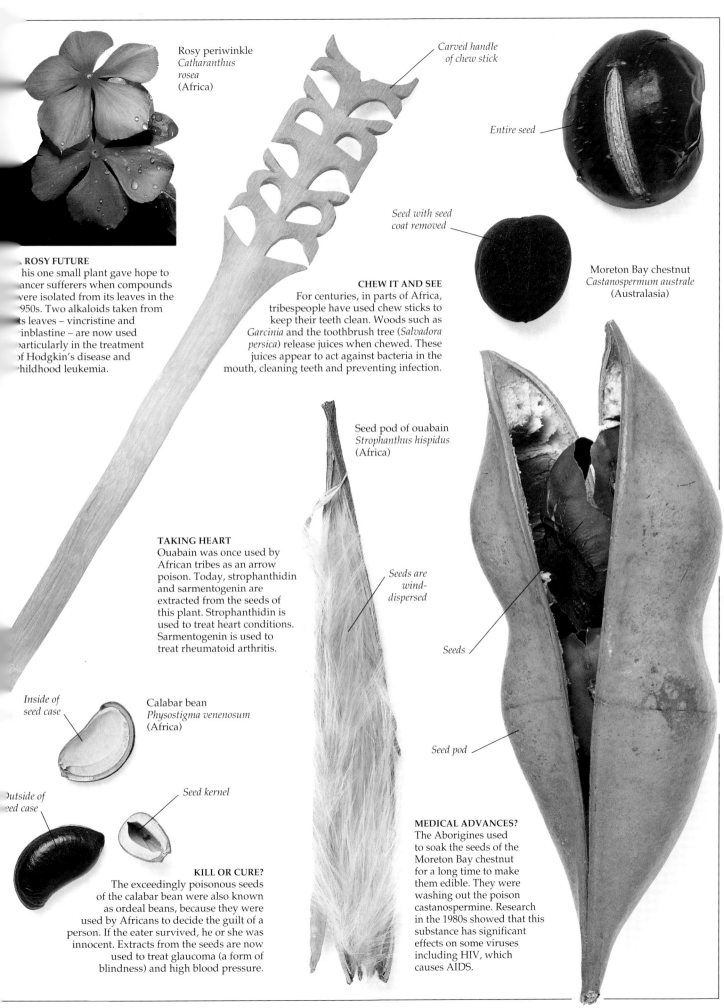

Rosy periwinkle
Catharanthus rosea
(Africa)

Carved handle of chew stick

Entire seed

Seed with seed coat removed

Moreton Bay chestnut
Castanospermum australe
(Australasia)

ROSY FUTURE
This one small plant gave hope to cancer sufferers when compounds were isolated from its leaves in the 1950s. Two alkaloids taken from its leaves – vincristine and vinblastine – are now used particularly in the treatment of Hodgkin's disease and childhood leukemia.

CHEW IT AND SEE
For centuries, in parts of Africa, tribespeople have used chew sticks to keep their teeth clean. Woods such as *Garcinia* and the toothbrush tree (*Salvadora persica*) release juices when chewed. These juices appear to act against bacteria in the mouth, cleaning teeth and preventing infection.

Seed pod of ouabain
Strophanthus hispidus
(Africa)

TAKING HEART
Ouabain was once used by African tribes as an arrow poison. Today, strophanthidin and sarmentogenin are extracted from the seeds of this plant. Strophanthidin is used to treat heart conditions. Sarmentogenin is used to treat rheumatoid arthritis.

Seeds are wind-dispersed

Seeds

Inside of seed case

Calabar bean
Physostigma venenosum
(Africa)

Seed kernel

Outside of seed case

Seed pod

KILL OR CURE?
The exceedingly poisonous seeds of the calabar bean were also known as ordeal beans, because they were used by Africans to decide the guilt of a person. If the eater survived, he or she was innocent. Extracts from the seeds are now used to treat glaucoma (a form of blindness) and high blood pressure.

MEDICAL ADVANCES?
The Aborigines used to soak the seeds of the Moreton Bay chestnut for a long time to make them edible. They were washing out the poison castanospermine. Research in the 1980s showed that this substance has significant effects on some viruses including HIV, which causes AIDS.

Forest apes

THE TROPICAL RAIN FORESTS are home to all of the world's apes, and most of its monkeys, although there are no primates in New Guinea and Australia. Many species are able to live close together because they inhabit different levels in the forest canopy, or eat different food. Even so, some groups are highly territorial: one of the lasting impressions of the jungle is the hollering and screeching of monkeys and apes defending their feeding area.

Very long arms

Jungle swinger

Gibbons like this siamang use their arms to swing from branch to branch. This process, called brachiation, is an effective way of moving very quickly through the forest canopy and is their usual means of locomotion. They do fall sometimes, with fatal results, but it is the most efficient way of finding the trees that have ripe fruit to eat. Although gibbons use brachiation most, chimpanzees and some monkeys also use this method.

Siamang
Hylobates syndactylus
(Southeast Asia)

Opposable big toe

GOING FOR A WALK
A gorilla moves around the forest floor on the flat of its feet and its knuckles in quest of the vast quantities of vegetation that it needs to eat every day. Although usually slow-moving, it is capable of bursts of speed when necessary, for example when chasing off a rival.

Gorilla
Gorilla gorilla
(Africa)

Gorillas have broad feet; the big toes are opposable so they can curl around to grip

Chimpanzees walk and climb in lower canopy, using both hands and feet

Gibbons spend all their time up in trees; they have narrow feet

JUNGLE CHORUS
The siamang is the largest of the gibbons. Each pair lives in the treetops with their offspring. They guard their territory and its vital food supply from neighboring siamangs with a morning and afternoon duet of ear-splitting shrieks and barks. The calls, which can be heard up to 0.6 miles (1 km) away, are given extra resonance by their inflated throat sacs.

Long, narrow hands with thumb cleft almost to the wrist

Forearm that can rotate 180°

Shoulder joint will rotate 360°

Powerful shoulder muscles

Leg outstretched to maximize forward movement

Broad chest

Legs curled up to increase upward stroke of swing

Legs shorter than arms

Long and opposable big toe

EVER CHIMP
...is primate is very good ...th its hands. Most ...impanzees use twigs ...get tasty morsels from ...fficult places, but some ...ack open nuts with ...ones or branches. They ...rry their "hammers" ...r long distances.

...himpanzee
...n troglodytes
...frica)

Mandrill
Mandrillus sphinx
(Africa)

Humboldt's monkey
Lagothrix lagotricha
(South America)

MONKEY ON THE MARCH
Male mandrills live mostly on the forest floor. Females and their young climb up into low undergrowth.

TAIL GRIP
Tree-dwelling woolly monkeys use their prehensile (grasping) tails to grip slippery branches in the canopy.

Hunters and killers

PREDATORS HAVE TO CATCH and kill other animals if they are to survive. They need to detect their prey before it notices them, to stalk, ambush, or outrun it before it escapes, and disable it before it can do them harm. To do all this, hunters must have keen senses. Daytime hunters often rely on their sharp eyesight to find prey. Nocturnal (nighttime) hunters need other skills – a highly developed sense of hearing or smell, or an ability to detect vibrations made by an approaching animal. Prey animals have their own defenses, such as camouflage, so an unlucky hunter goes hungry.

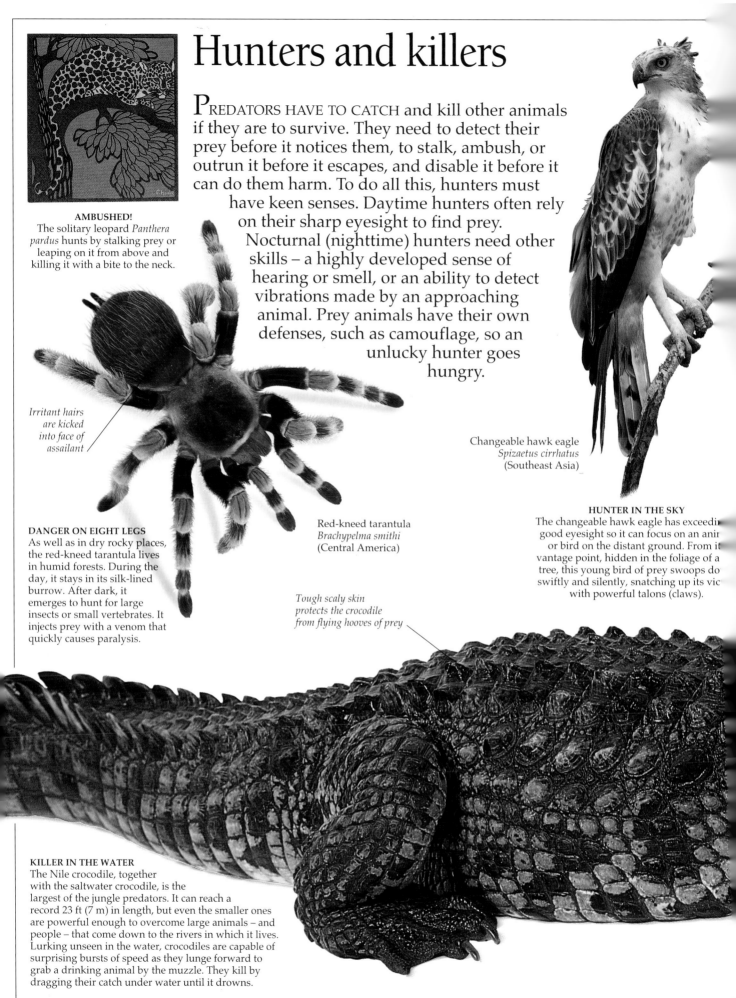

AMBUSHED!
The solitary leopard *Panthera pardus* hunts by stalking prey or leaping on it from above and killing it with a bite to the neck.

Irritant hairs are kicked into face of assailant

DANGER ON EIGHT LEGS
As well as in dry rocky places, the red-kneed tarantula lives in humid forests. During the day, it stays in its silk-lined burrow. After dark, it emerges to hunt for large insects or small vertebrates. It injects prey with a venom that quickly causes paralysis.

Red-kneed tarantula
Brachypelma smithi
(Central America)

Changeable hawk eagle
Spizaetus cirrhatus
(Southeast Asia)

HUNTER IN THE SKY
The changeable hawk eagle has exceedi[n]g good eyesight so it can focus on an ani[mal] or bird on the distant ground. From i[ts] vantage point, hidden in the foliage of a tree, this young bird of prey swoops do[wn] swiftly and silently, snatching up its vic[tim] with powerful talons (claws).

Tough scaly skin protects the crocodile from flying hooves of prey

KILLER IN THE WATER
The Nile crocodile, together with the saltwater crocodile, is the largest of the jungle predators. It can reach a record 23 ft (7 m) in length, but even the smaller ones are powerful enough to overcome large animals – and people – that come down to the rivers in which it lives. Lurking unseen in the water, crocodiles are capable of surprising bursts of speed as they lunge forward to grab a drinking animal by the muzzle. They kill by dragging their catch under water until it drowns.

SMALL BUT DEADLY
The Southern fer-de-lance is nocturnal and locates warm-blooded prey with heat-sensitive pits between its eyes and nostrils. When a victim is in range, this viper gapes open its mouth, and two long front fangs swing forward. As the snake strikes, these fangs stab, injecting a lethal venom. Most human deaths from snake bites in South America are due to this species.

...e lures
...th
...ail

Southern fer-de-lance
Bothrops atrox
(South America)

SQUEEZED TO DEATH
The boa constrictor waits motionless until its prey comes close. The animal's air-borne scent is picked up by the snake's tongue and transferred to the sensitive Jacobson's organs on the roof of its mouth. The snake strikes open-mouthed, gripping its catch with its fangs and coiling around the animal's body. Each time the animal breathes out, the snake tightens its coils a little more, until the prey is suffocated.

...constrictor
...onstrictor
...tral and South
...erica)

*Powerful jaws
to swallow
large prey*

*Formidable array of sharp teeth
that are replaced continuously
throughout the crocodile's life*

Nile crocodile
Crocodylus niloticus
(Africa)

*Strong claws to
climb quickly up
slippery riverbanks*

TOOTH AND CLAW
The tiger *Panthera tigris* is a solitary animal that hunts by day or night. The tiger stalks a victim, pouncing on it with formidably clawed forepaws and killing it with a bite to the neck. A tiger's usual diet is deer, goats, and sometimes large cattle. Some tigers, particularly old or injured animals, will go after anything, including people.

Tropical Asia

THE TERM "JUNGLE" is derived from the Hindi word *jangal*, meaning impenetrable forest and undergrowth. Tropical Asia includes many countries and encompasses an enormous area. Part of this is continental mainland, but stretching southeast of this area are the archipelagos (island groups) of Indonesia and Malaysia, some large, others tiny. It is a diverse and complex region, with many different peoples and histories. Much of the land is covered with tropical forest, including montane forests and the evergreen and monsoon forests of the lowlands, all of which are rich in plant and animal life. With so much coastline, it's not surprising that most of the world's mangrove swamps are found here.

Prominent eyes with vertical pupils for seeing in low light

WORKING WITH PLA
Palm trees provide a plen raw material for many industries. This Sarawak g splitting palm leaves into strip be woven into matting or bas

TREE SNAKE
The nocturnal green cat snake (*Boiga cyanea*) lives almost exclusively in trees, often near water. It preys on other arboreal (tree-dwelling) creatures, such as tree frogs and lizards. After paralyzing its prey with venom from fangs at the back of its mouth, the snake swallows it whole.

INDIA

Bay of Bengal

China Sea

Malaysia

Indonesia

☐ *Former rain forest*
☐ *Actual rain forest*

Malayan tapir
Tapirus indicus

INDIA AND SOUTHEAST AS
Many generations of huma inhabitants have left little of t forest of mainland Southeast Asia its natural state. Some countrie such as Vietnam, are replantin Some islands, notably in th Philippines, have lost all their rai forests. Others, such as Borneo, st retain most of their original fore cover, parts of which are sti unknown to outsider

BROWSER
The tapir is a solitary animal that is most active at night. With its long movable snout, it browses through leaves, fruits, and seeds in the thick jungle growth bordering water.

Strong legs for swimming

48

tan palm
amus caesius

AN PALMS
are about 600
s of rattans. These
mbing palms that
the canopy by
s of whips on the
the fronds; these
are covered with
d spikes. Rattan
are commercially
tant for making
ure that is exported
ound the world.

*Shape of petals
attracts insects*

*Stem can reach
over 660 ft
(200 m) in length*

*Leaf sheath covered
in hooked spines*

ONE OF THE FEW
There are about 70 species of
tropical slipper orchid, all of
which are found in Southeast
Asia. Most of them grow on the
ground, but a few grow on trees
or rocks. Many slipper orchids are
naturally rare because they have
specific habitat requirements.
Since 1964, 20 new species have
been described, and *Paphiopedilum
primulinum* itself was only
discovered in 1972.

ver bud

Slipper orchid
*Paphiopedilum
primulinum*

THE GINGER LILY
Many ginger lilies (*Hedychium* spp.) have fragrant,
attractive flowers, and their thick underground stems
often contain aromatic (nice-smelling) oils. After the
tubular flower wilts, a fruit capsule develops. When
this is ripe, it splits to reveal three rows of seeds.

Disguise and warning

ANIMALS AND INSECTS use camouflage in an effort to avoid being eaten. Color and shape either make an animal indistinguishable from its background, or trick a predator into thinking that it is dealing with something bigger or more dangerous. Animals with cryptic coloration have colors or patterns that closely match their background. Some patterns seem bold and conspicuous, but they actually make it impossible to see the animal against a mosaic of leaves, twigs, sunshine, and shadow by breaking up the animal's outline. Mimicry takes this kind of camouflage a stage further, in insects that look like leaves, bark, or twigs. The disguise of many insects is so good that, rather than waste time looking for them, flocks of several species of birds will move noisily through the forest like a wave. What small creatures one bird dislodges or disturbs, the bird behind snaps up.

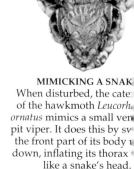

MIMICKING A SNAK[E]
When disturbed, the cate[rpillar] of the hawkmoth *Leucorh[...] ornatus* mimics a small ver[...] pit viper. It does this by sw[...] the front part of its body u[...] down, inflating its thorax [...] like a snake's head.

False leaf katydid
Ommatopia pictifolia
(Central America)

STARTLE DISPLAY
The forewings of the false leaf katydid are near-perfect replicas of dead leaves. When motionless, it blends in well with low-growing vegetation. However, if it is discovered, this katydid has a second line of defense. In one quick movement, the forewings part to reveal a startling display of eyespots. This display should scare a predator long enough for the katydid to escape.

CHANGING COLOR
The chameleon's colors intensify, with spots and stripes of purple rapidly appearing. His tail straightens, and he takes up a more aggressive stance, pu[...] up his body to make it look bigger.

Parson's chameleon
Chamaeleo parsonii
(Africa)

REACTION TIME
Contrary to popular belief, a male chameleon does not change colour to match different backgrounds. But at the sight of a rival entering his territory, the response is immediate.

*ach eye swivels
*dependently,
*o the chameleon
*an look in two
*irections at the
ame time

COLOR CHANGE IN CHAMELEONS

The skin of chameleons contains a small range of colored pigments in specialized cells called chromatophores. Those that contain black pigment (melanin) lie deeper in the skin. When facing an intruder, a hormone is released from the pituitary gland. This hormone triggers a surge of melanin pigment to the surface of the skin, and the skin color darkens.

DARKER AND DARKER

His color is now at its most intense. The red eyes and patches of red and green stand out against the deep blackish purple. In an attempt to scare away the intruder, he hisses and lunges forward.

Warning coloration

Some poisonous animals and insects are conspicuously marked with bright colors and striking patterns that warn would-be predators, usually birds, that they taste awful. Often, the strategy is copied by non-poisonous species. It is known as Batesian mimicry, after Henry Walter Bates, the man who first described it. A change of color is also used to communicate with a member of the same species. It can reflect a change of mood, scare off a rival, or signal to a potential mate during the breeding season.

Tiger moth
Ormeticia temporata
(Central America)

ALTERNATIVE DEFENSE

Unlike many other insects, moths and butterflies cannot sting attackers, or defend themselves by biting. Instead, they have other methods. This tiger moth is well protected by its bold warning coloration. The bright yellow stripes on the wings act to discourage or frighten predators.

CAMOUFLAGED CAT

Light-colored fur with dark stripes, spots, or blotches imitates the dappled effect of sunlight in the dense vegetation of the rain forest. It makes an effective camouflage for jungle cats. Tigers rely on their ability to remain unseen as they stalk an intended victim, until they are close enough to pounce.

Tricks and traps

AT ALL LEVELS of the rain forest, there is a host of alert, wary creatures with a strong instinct for survival. A predator always has to outsmart its prey if it is to catch enough to eat. Some hunters combine trickery and deception with patience and the ability to move at lightning speed. Plants have a few tricks of their own. Sap-sucking insects may have their mouthparts gummed up by an unexpected flow of sticky latex. Plants that grow on poor or peaty soils cannot get enough nutrients. In order to survive, some of these plants have turned into carnivores.

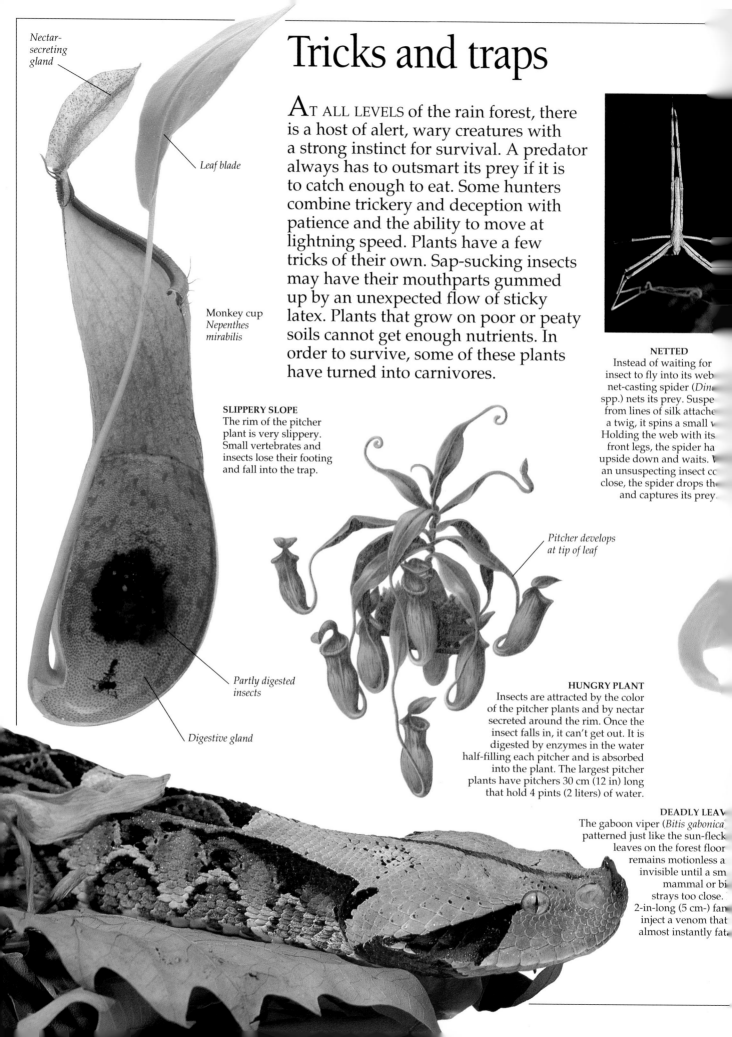

Nectar-secreting gland

Leaf blade

Monkey cup
Nepenthes mirabilis

SLIPPERY SLOPE
The rim of the pitcher plant is very slippery. Small vertebrates and insects lose their footing and fall into the trap.

Partly digested insects

Digestive gland

NETTED
Instead of waiting for insect to fly into its web net-casting spider (*Dine spp.) nets its prey. Suspe from lines of silk attache a twig, it spins a small w Holding the web with its front legs, the spider ha upside down and waits. an unsuspecting insect co close, the spider drops th and captures its prey.

Pitcher develops at tip of leaf

HUNGRY PLANT
Insects are attracted by the color of the pitcher plants and by nectar secreted around the rim. Once the insect falls in, it can't get out. It is digested by enzymes in the water half-filling each pitcher and is absorbed into the plant. The largest pitcher plants have pitchers 30 cm (12 in) long that hold 4 pints (2 liters) of water.

DEADLY LEAV
The gaboon viper (*Bitis gabonica* patterned just like the sun-fleck leaves on the forest floor remains motionless a invisible until a sm mammal or bi strays too close. 2-in-long (5 cm-) fan inject a venom that almost instantly fat

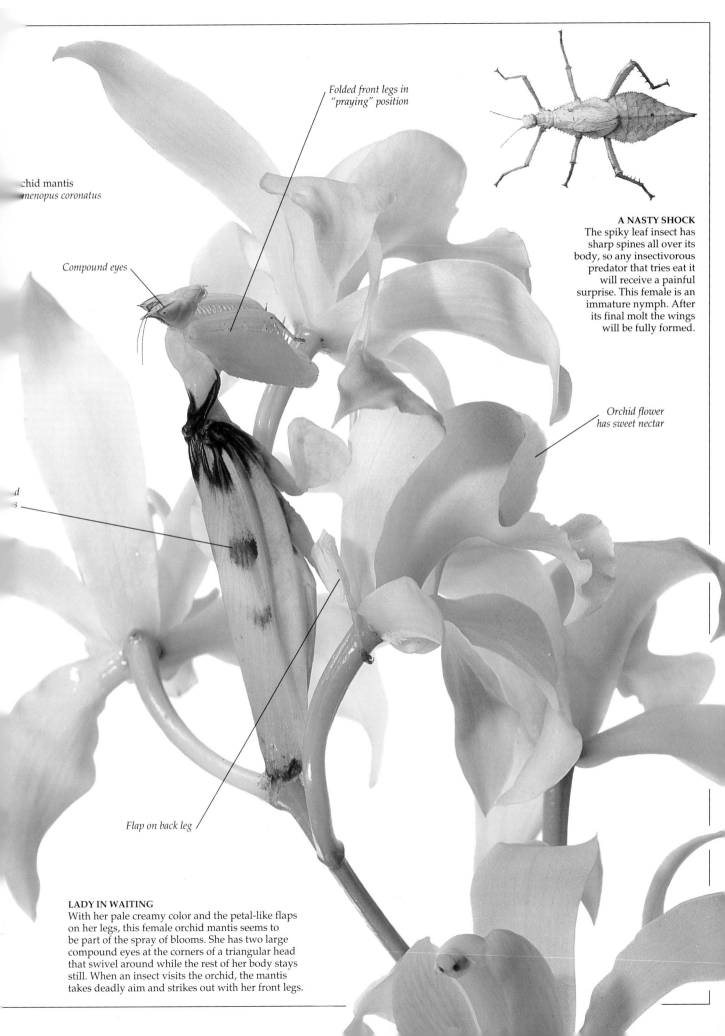

Orchid mantis
Hymenopus coronatus

Folded front legs in
"praying" position

Compound eyes

Flap on back leg

A NASTY SHOCK
The spiky leaf insect has
sharp spines all over its
body, so any insectivorous
predator that tries eat it
will receive a painful
surprise. This female is an
immature nymph. After
its final molt the wings
will be fully formed.

Orchid flower
has sweet nectar

LADY IN WAITING
With her pale creamy color and the petal-like flaps
on her legs, this female orchid mantis seems to
be part of the spray of blooms. She has two large
compound eyes at the corners of a triangular head
that swivel around while the rest of her body stays
still. When an insect visits the orchid, the mantis
takes deadly aim and strikes out with her front legs.

Flying high

FROG BEETLE
This Malayan frog beetle (*Sagra buqueti*) has its wings folded under wing cases called elytra.

BEETLING ABOUT
Before flying, this leaf beetle (*Doryphorella langsdorfii*) opens its elytra and spreads its wings.

SOMETIMES AN ANIMAL needs to travel from treetop to treetrop in search of food or to escape a predator. Running down one tree trunk, along the ground, and up the next is hazardous and a waste of energy. Traveling through the air overcomes this, but only birds, bats, and insects have the wings and muscles that permit controlled flight. However, an assortment of other creatures have evolved ways of gliding through the air by increasing their body area, often with flaps of skin. When airborne, these flaps spread out like parachutes, increasing the animal's wind resistance and slowing down the rate of descent preventing a damaging collision with the ground below! Many of these gliders can change direction in midair by moving their legs, tail, or body, and some travel remarkable distances in this way.

BIRDS OF PARADISE
The splendid plumage of male birds of paradise is used simply to attract a mate. Males gather in groups called leks in order to display. Some choose a high treetop and, as day breaks, give a colorful display, flashing their bright, iridescent plumage while making loud calls.

FLYING GECKO
This nocturnal gecko (*Ptychozoon kuhli*) lives in trees and relies on camouflage to hide it from predators. If it is spotted, it escapes by launching itself into the air and gliding to safety. Loose flaps of skin along each side of its body, and smaller flaps on its legs, spread out and fill with air.

Wide scales along tail

Flaps make lizard wider and flatter for gliding

Long legs for running

Webbing between toes

FLYING FROG
The Malaysian flying frog (*Rhacophorus reinwardii*) is one of a small number of rain forest tree frogs that leap out of a tree to escape from a pursuer. The digits of their very large hands and feet are connected by webs of skin. During long gliding leaps, these webs of skin serve as parachutes.

HUNTING WASP
The electric blue female hunting wasp (*Chlorion lobatum*) cruises low over the forest floor, hunting for crickets. It grips its prey with powerful jaws and paralyzes it with venom injected by its stinger. It drags the insect into a burrow and lays a single egg in it so that, on hatching, the larva has food until it pupates.

Blue-and-yellow macaw
Ara ararauna
(South America)

EXPERT PILOTS
Macaws have short, broad wings
so that they can skillfully maneuver
between the leafy branches of the forest canopy.
They fly considerable distances in search of trees
bearing ripe fruits. By changing the position of their
wings and tail feathers, they can glide and brake
before landing on a branch or at a tree-hole nesting site.

FLYING SNAKE
The flying tree snake (*Chrysopelea
pelias*) is one of five species from
Southeast Asia that can glide through
the air. By raising its ribs upward and
outward, the snake flattens its body and
manages to travel distances of up to 165
ft (50 m) from one tree to another.

Flying
dragon
Draco spp.

FLYING LIZARD
Flying dragons have six or
seven pairs of elongated ribs
covered with a membrane of
skin. These "wings" fold up
against the lizard's body,
but open out so it can glide
long distances.

ing
tern and
ors help
les and
nales find
ch other

GIANT MOTH
The Atlas moth (*Attacus atlas*) is
one of the largest moths, with a
wingspan of 10-12 in (25-30 cm).
Unlike those of other insects, the wings
of moths and butterflies are covered
with minute, overlapping scales. These
are richly colored, some because they
contain colored pigments, others
because of the way that they reflect
the light that falls on them.

Australasian rain forests

ONE HUNDRED MILLION years ago, Australia was part of Antarctica, and rain forest covered the moist coastal regions of this vast southern continent. As Australia separated and drifted north, it became drier, and Antarctica colder. Australia's rain forests are all that is left of this ancient jungle, and contain some primitive flowering plants and conifers. Apart from the bats, all the native animals are pouch-bearing marsupials. New Guinea is to the north, a heavily forested island with a mixture of Asian and Australian plants and animals.

DANGER UNDERFOOT
The marbled scorpion (*Lychas marmoreus*) is found under bark and among leaf litter, where it hunts for small invertebrates. It usually overpowers its victim with its front claws and jaws. The venomous sting in the tail is used primarily for defense.

GREEN AND RED
The tiny flowers of this fig (*Ficus racemosus*) are contained in the fleshy green swellings that will eventually become sweet fruits. When the figs ripen, they turn red.

RARE AND BEAUTIFUL
Living only in a small area of the extreme southeast of Papua New Guinea, this is one of the world's rarest butterflies. It is also the largest—the female has a wingspan of up to 11 in (28 cm). These butterflies are found in the forest margins, but little is known about them.

The male is smaller than the female

Queen Alexandra's birdwing
Ornithoptera alexandrae

IN THE SHADE
This fleshy-stemmed fern lives beside water in shady forests. There is little strengthening tissue in the leaf stalks, and they soon wilt in dry conditions. *Angiopteris* ferns are very similar to the primitive ferns and tree ferns that were alive 325 to 280 million years ago, in the Upper Carboniferous period.

Long, arching leaf stalk

Marattia fern
Angiopteris lygodiifolia

SOGERI SING-SING
In Papua New Guinea elaborate rituals and ceremonies such as the sing-sing have always been an important part of tribal life. New Guinea men adorn themselves with brightly colored body paints, feathers, shells, and beads. Head dresses made with bird of paradise feathers are especially prestigious.

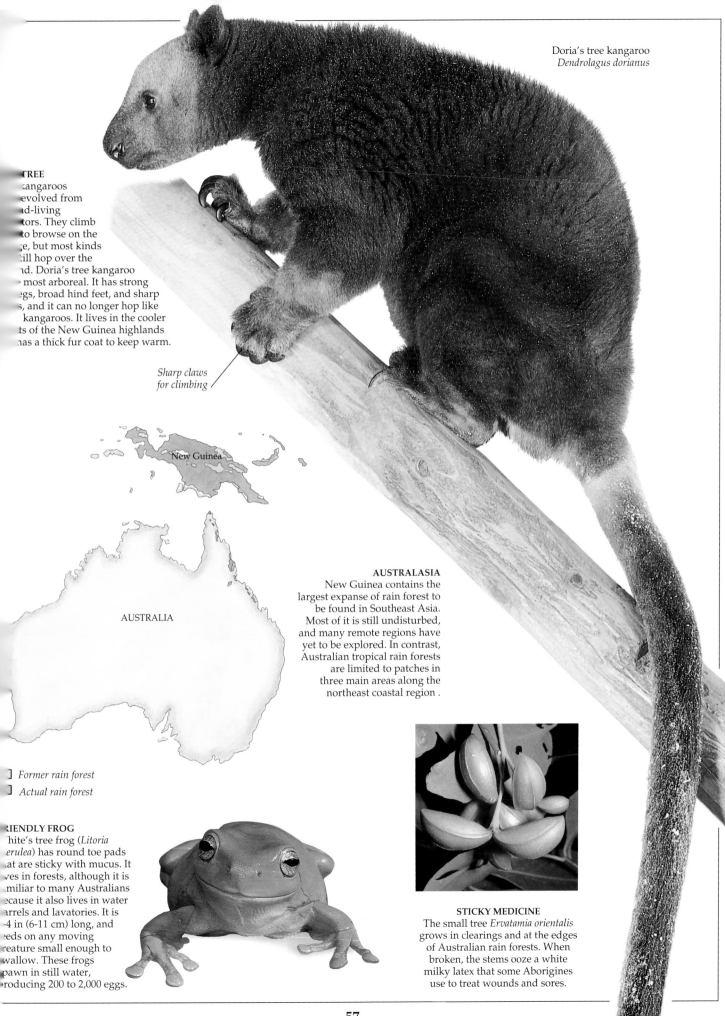

Doria's tree kangaroo
Dendrolagus dorianus

...TREE
...kangaroos
...evolved from
...d-living
...ors. They climb
...o browse on the
...e, but most kinds
...ill hop over the
...nd. Doria's tree kangaroo
...e most arboreal. It has strong
...gs, broad hind feet, and sharp
..., and it can no longer hop like
... kangaroos. It lives in the cooler
...ts of the New Guinea highlands
...as a thick fur coat to keep warm.

*Sharp claws
for climbing*

New Guinea

AUSTRALIA

AUSTRALASIA
New Guinea contains the
largest expanse of rain forest to
be found in Southeast Asia.
Most of it is still undisturbed,
and many remote regions have
yet to be explored. In contrast,
Australian tropical rain forests
are limited to patches in
three main areas along the
northeast coastal region .

] *Former rain forest*
] *Actual rain forest*

...RIENDLY FROG
...hite's tree frog (*Litoria
...erulea*) has round toe pads
...at are sticky with mucus. It
...ves in forests, although it is
...miliar to many Australians
...ecause it also lives in water
...arrels and lavatories. It is
...-4 in (6-11 cm) long, and
...eds on any moving
...reature small enough to
...wallow. These frogs
...pawn in still water,
...roducing 200 to 2,000 eggs.

STICKY MEDICINE
The small tree *Ervatamia orientalis*
grows in clearings and at the edges
of Australian rain forests. When
broken, the stems ooze a white
milky latex that some Aborigines
use to treat wounds and sores.

Jungle produce

For many centuries, jungle products have been carried all around the world. A few, such as rubber, sugar, and chocolate, are now so much a part of everyday life it is easy to forget their rain forest origins. Products sold all over the world are grown mostly in plantations. However, some, such as Brazil nuts, are still gathered from the forest. Many of the fruits and seeds that the native peoples have enjoyed for a long time are only now beginning to find new markets in North America and Europe. In the future, we may be enjoying ice creams and using cosmetics that contain ever more exotic ingredients from the jungle.

NUTMEG PLANT
The red aril around the nutmeg seed is also used as a spice called mace.

A POPULAR FLAVOR
Over 1,227,000 tons of cocoa beans are produced every year to manufacture chocolate, cocoa, and cocoa butter.

SPICING IT UP
Strongly flavored spices such as pepper, ginger, cloves, and nutmeg were highly prized and very expensive in Europe in the Middle Ages. They were used to hide the tainted flavor of bad meat. Today they are used to enhance the flavor of food, and to make medicines and toothpastes taste better. Spices are prepared from different parts of plants. For example, nutmeg is a seed, cloves are unopened flower buds, cinnamon comes from the bark, and ginger is a root. They are dried and can be ground into a powder.

Gi
Zin
offic

Cloves
Syzygium aromaticum

Nutmeg
Myristica fragrans

Cinnam
Cinnamon
zeylanic

COCOA BEANS
Cocoa trees have been cultivated for over 2,000 years in Central America. The Aztecs called the po "cacahual," and believ that Quetzalcoatl, the plumed serpent god, dined on them. When ripe, cocoa pods are c and split open by han The wet, pulpy mass of seeds is piled into baskets and allowed to ferment to lose unwanted pulp and develop the flavor. Then the seeds – the cocoa beans – are dried, cleaned, and polished, ready for export.

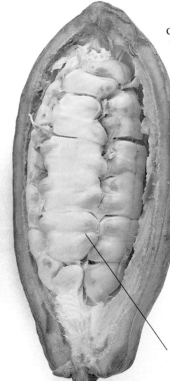

Cocoa pod
Theobroma cacao

Pulp

Rows of 20-60 oval seeds are embedded in a sweet pulp

Starfruit
Averrhoa carambola

Pineapple
Ananas comosus

STARFRUIT
Starfruits grow wild in Indonesian forests, but are planted widely in tropical Asia. They are an attractive garnish on food, as well as a source of vitamin C and iron.

ET POTATO
starchy root (*Ipomoea
as*) originated in tropical
erica and contains sugars,
is pleasantly sweet. Sweet
toes are boiled, roasted,
ried and ground into flour.

ADFRUIT
mass of flowers on
plant develop into
breadfruit, which is
in (20-30 cm) across
can weigh as much
lb 4 oz (2 kg). Its
st, starchy flesh
oked as a
etable.

RUBBER
Over 1,000 kinds of plants produce the white, sticky latex that can be made into rubber. The para rubber tree (*Hevea brasiliensis*) is by far the most commonly used.

*Pineapple
cloth, or piña*

PINEAPPLE
Originating in South America, pineapples are now grown in many tropical countries. Both fresh and canned pineapples are popular foods, but the leaves have a different use. In the Philippines, thin fibers are extracted, prepared, spun, and woven by hand to make a fine sheer cloth called piña. Piña shirts are part of the national costume.

Breadfruit
Artocarpus altilis

Large, sturdy prehensile tail

Explorers

THE PROFITABLE spice market drew Portuguese, English, and Dutch explorers to the forested islands of Southeast Asia in the 15th, 16th, and 17th centuries. At the same time, Spanish conquistadors were exploring Central America and Peru, interested more in ransacking Aztec and Inca gold than in the jungles. From the 16th century onward, rival European nations fought to extend their empires in tropical regions. The 18th and 19th centuries saw a steady rise in scientific curiosity about these areas, with explorers such as Darwin and Wallace evolving the theories that have shaped modern thinking.

WILLIAM BLIGH (1754-1817)
For explorers who sailed the sea bygone days, conditions were ha In 1789, Captain Bligh was skipp the *Bounty*, commissioned to tran young breadfruit trees from the is of Tahiti to the West Indies. His c who wanted to stay on Tahiti, reb and the famous mutiny took plac second attempt to deliver the tre succeeded and one, planted by B on St. Vincent, is still standing

AIMÉ BONPLAND (1773-1858)
With von Humboldt, the Frenchman Aimé Bonpland explored both montane and lowland rain forests. Bonpland was a gifted artist and botanist, and recorded over 3,000 new species of plant, such as this *Melastoma coccinea*, in a splendid series of paintings.

Simia ursina painted by Alexander von Humbol

ALEXAND VON HUMBOL (1769-18
This German natura landed in Venezuela in 17 with Bonpland. Von Humbo had a keen scientific inter in the animals, plan and places discovere

IT'S ALL IN THE NAME
This woolly monkey, *Lagothrix lagotricha* (left), comes from the Orinoco and Upper Amazon basins. It is often called Humboldt's monkey to commemorate the intrepid explorer, who had to put up with swarms of biting insects and fevers in this very humid region.

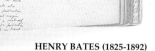

Pages from one of Bates's notebooks

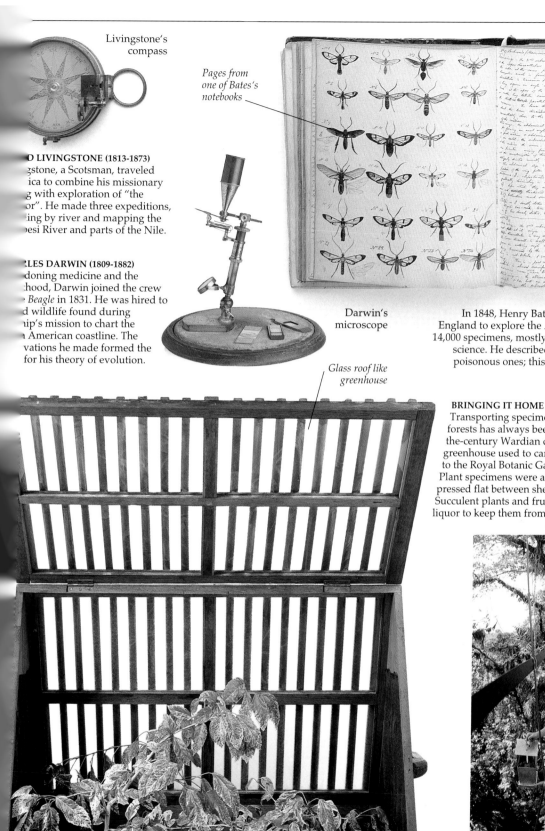

DAVID LIVINGSTONE (1813-1873)

Livingstone, a Scotsman, traveled [Afr]ica to combine his missionary [calling] with exploration of "the [interi]or". He made three expeditions, [travel]ing by river and mapping the [Zamb]esi River and parts of the Nile.

CHARLES DARWIN (1809-1882)

[Aban]doning medicine and the [priest]hood, Darwin joined the crew [of the] *Beagle* in 1831. He was hired to [record] wildlife found during [the sh]ip's mission to chart the [South] American coastline. The [obser]vations he made formed the [basis] for his theory of evolution.

Darwin's microscope

Glass roof like greenhouse

HENRY BATES (1825-1892)

In 1848, Henry Bates and his friend Alfred Wallace left England to explore the Amazon. In 11 years, Bates collected 14,000 specimens, mostly insects, of which 8,000 were new to science. He described how some harmless species mimic poisonous ones; this is now known as Batesian mimicry.

BRINGING IT HOME

Transporting specimens back from the rain forests has always been difficult. This turn-of-the-century Wardian case (left) is a portable greenhouse used to carry plants safely back to the Royal Botanic Gardens at Kew, England. Plant specimens were also preserved by being pressed flat between sheets of absorbent paper. Succulent plants and fruits were preserved in liquor to keep them from becoming moldy.

YOUNG VENTURER

Since the 1970s, Colonel John Blashford-Snell has probably done most to enable biologists and young people called Venturers to investigate the canopy. In Operations Drake and Raleigh, the biologists and Venturers studied plants and animals from lightweight aluminium walkways many feet above the ground.

Under threat

EVERY MINUTE OF THE DAY, 100 acres (40 hectares) of tropical rain forest are destroyed. At present, rain forests cover about 6% of the Earth's surface – half the area covered at the beginning of the 20th century – and the rate of clearance is increasing. The trees are felled for logs, burned to make way for farming, and polluted by mining. New roads have opened up previously inaccessible regions, and settlers clear the land to grow crops. If the clearance continues, 15% of plant species and 12% of bird species could become extinct in American forests alone by the year 2000.

CLEARANCE FOR CATTLE RANCHING
In South and Central America, cleared tropical rain forest provides pasture for beef cattle, the numbers of which rose from 1 million in 1970 to 5.5 million in 1985. After five years, each animal needs 12.5 acres (5 hectares) to graze. After ten years the land is useless. Overgrazing, the impact of the animals' hooves, and the loss of the trees lead to soil erosion.

ENVIRONMENTAL INFLUENCES
Rain forests influence the carbon cycle and also have a profound effect on rainfall. The uneven surface of treetops causes air turbulence that increases the amount of water evaporating from the forest. This water forms clouds and falls as rain. If the forests disappear, less rain will fall, it will drain more quickly, and air and soil temperatures will rise.

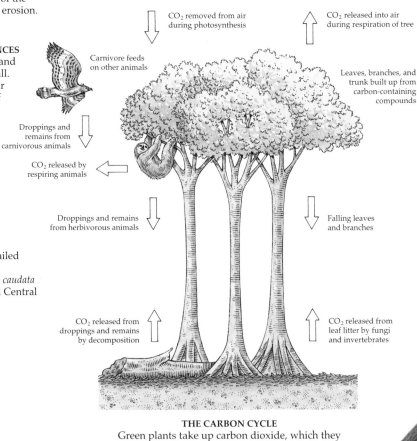

CO₂ removed from air during photosynthesis

CO₂ released into air during respiration of tree

Carnivore feeds on other animals

Leaves, branches, and trunk built up from carbon-containing compounds

Droppings and remains from carnivorous animals

CO₂ released by respiring animals

Droppings and remains from herbivorous animals

Falling leaves and branches

CO₂ released from droppings and remains by decomposition

CO₂ released from leaf litter by fungi and invertebrates

Swallow-tailed manakin
Chiroxiphia caudata
(South and Central America)

THE CARBON CYCLE
Green plants take up carbon dioxide, which they convert to sugars by means of photosynthesis. During this process, oxygen is released into the air.

THE OLD AND THE NEW
This beautiful Dutch mahogany armoire is an antique. Today, most of the mahogany that comes from Amazonia is poached – felled illegally – at the expense of the lives and livelihood of the Amerindian tribespeople.

VULNERABLE
Manakins live in the thickest forests and are not endangered at present. But their lifestyle and specialized diet of small soft fruits makes them vulnerable to forest disturbance.

Maxillaria fulgens (Central America)

OBSESSIVE COLLECTION
Many of the estimated 18,000 species of orchid are found in rain forests. Their exotic blooms attract collectors, and the trade in these flowers, although frequently illegal, is worth a lot of money. Orchids are highly susceptible to over-collection, and some face extinction in the wild.

WIGMAN OF THE HULI TRIBE
Papua New Guinea has some of the least disturbed areas of rain forest. Many tribes live there, but the harmony with their surroundings is easily disrupted.

BROIDERED CLOTH, NILGIRI HILLS
he Nilgiri Hills, in India, a large area orest has been made into a Biosphere erve. Tribal groups are encouraged ive there in a traditional way, and y supplement their livelihood making items for export.

Orangutan
Pongo pygmaeus
(Southeast Asia)

Arms are much longer than legs

rt fifth toe to grip branches en swinging

NOWHERE TO LIVE
Selective logging removes target trees but leaves the rest. The increased light stimulates new growth, which benefits some animals, such as leaf-eating primates that prefer young foliage. Others are not so adaptable. The adult orangutan forages over a wide area on its own and is highly sensitive to disturbance. Like all other jungle creatures, this "man of the forest" has a right to survive.

Index

Acknowledgments

Dorling Kindersley would like to thank:
Mark Alcock; the staff of the Royal Botanic Gardens, Kew, in particular Jenny Evans, Doris Francis, Sandra Bell, Phil Brewster, Dave Cooke, John Lonsdale, Mike Marsh, and John Norris; David Field and Sue Brodie of ECOS, the Royal Botanic Gardens, Kew; Mark O'Shea, herpetologist, and Nik Brown and Pete Montague of the West Midland Safari Park; the staff and keepers of Twycross Zoo, in particular Molly Badham, Donna Chester, and John Ray; Robert Opie, Jim Hamill, Jane Beamish, and Mike Row, British Museum, Museum of Mankind; Martin Brendell of the Natural History Museum; Janet Boston of the Liverpool Museum; Helena Spiteri

for editorial help; Susan St Louis, Isaac Zamora, Ivan Finnegan, and Sarah Cowley for design help.
Maps by John Woodcock
Additional photography by Peter Anderson (38-39); Geoff Brightling (33tr); Jane Burton/Kim Taylor (17cl and cr, 33cl); Peter Chadwick (16cr); Frank Greenaway (12tl, 23tr and br, 28tl and bl, 29tl, 35cl, 37r, 52b, 53b, 54c, 55b, 56cr); Colin Keates (7cr, 54tl); Dave King (58b); Cyril Laubscher (7tr); Karl Shone (32-33, 62bl); Kim Taylor (40tr, 50-51); Jerry Young (16cl, 17b, 23br, 29bl, 31tr, 35tl, 53tr, 63b)
Index by Hilary Bird

Picture credits

a=above, b=below, c=center, l=left, r=right, t=top
Bridgeman Art Library/Royal Botanic

Gardens, Kew: 18bl, 35c; /Leiden, Rijksmuseum voor Volkenkunde: 38 bc; /British Museum: 39tr; /Royal Geographical Society: 60br; /Bonhams: 62bc
Bruce Coleman Ltd: 9tl; /M.P.L.Fogden: 12tr; /G.B.Frith: 15tl; /Konrad Wothe: 16c; /Jane Burton: 27tl; /D.Houston: 28br; /WWF/H.Jungins: 33tl; /Dieter and Mary Plage: 36bl; /Peter Ward: 37bl; /Dieter and Mary Plage: 46tr
Mary Evans Picture Library: 46tl
Michael & Patricia Fogden: 6bc, 13br, 13bl, 14c, 14tr, 35tr, 51bl, 63tr
Robert Harding Picture Library: 30lc, 34tr, 39tl, 62tl, 63tc
Hutchison Library/Isabella Tree: 39br; /Dr Nigel Smith: 42br
Frank Lane Picture Agency/E.& D. Hosking: 11tl; /Silvestris: 31bl
Mansell Collection: 60tr
Natural History Museum, London: 59
N.H.P.A./Morten Strange: 8tl; /Otto Rogge: 15r; /Stephen Dalton: 24cr, 33cr; /Kevin Schafer: 43tl; /G.I.Bernard: 50cr; /Stephen Kraseman: 50tr

Planet Earth Pictures/Andre Bartschi: 8bl; /Peter Scoones: 9tr; /Andrew Mounter: 21tl; /John Lythgoe: 22bl; /Anup Shah: 47br; /David Maitland: 56tr; /Mary Clay: 57bc
Premaphotos Wildlife/K.G.Preston-Mafham: 49br, 56lc, 57br
Raleigh International Picture Library/Chris Rainier: 61br
Harry Smith/Polunin Collection: 10tr
Still Pictures/Edward Parker: 6tl; /Norbert Wu: 29tr, 52tr
Survival Anglia/Frances Furlong: 40bc; /M.Kavanagh: 48tr
Syndication International: 58tl; /Natural History Museum: 60cr
c.Alan Watson/Forest Light: 8cr
M.I.Walker/Microworld Services: 18bc

Every effort has been made to trace the copyright holders and we apologize in advance for any unintentional omissions. We would be pleased to insert the appropriate acknowledgement in any subsequent edition of this publication.